Pancakes
make people happy

OVER
75
RECIPES

Sharon Collins, Charlotte Collins & Courtney Wade

Hatherleigh Press is committed to preserving and protecting the natural resources of the earth. Environmentally responsible and sustainable practices are embraced within the company's mission statement. Visit us at www.hatherleighpress.com and register online for free offers, discounts, special events, and more.

Pancakes Make People Happy

Text Copyright © 2021 Sharon Collins, Charlotte Collins and Courtney Wade

Library of Congress Cataloging-in-Publication Data is available.

ISBN: 978-1-57826-875-7

Book design by Carolyn Kasper

Printed in the United States

10 9 8 7 6 5 4 3 2 1

Contents

A Pancake Preface   vii

Pancakes 101: How to Use This Book   x

Easy Substitutions   xiii

• The Recipes •

Classic Pancakes   3

Savory Pancakes   25

Brunch Pancakes   51

International Pancakes   73

Seasonal Pancakes   95

Dessert Pancakes   121

A Pancake By Any Other Name   153

Closing Words   169

About the Authors   171

About Buck Hill Farm   173

Index   175

A Pancake Preface

Welcome to our pancake book. Since the beginning of time, when cavemen poured mashed grains on hot stones, pancakes have been a "go to" for filling up bellies and getting energy for the day. In the eons since, it has been customary to leave pitchers of batter next to stoves in kitchens of all walks of life, just waiting for a hungry bunch to awaken. The essence of this anticipation brings joy, and pancakes fuel the happiness. In this day and age, with no-carb and low-carb diets, pancakes get a bad rap. We hope to convince our audience that pancakes can be healthy and nourishing; that they lend themselves well to any diet restrictions; and most of all. that pancakes can find a home at any time, with any meal! As we say, "Move over charcuterie!", plan your next event around a pancake board!

Two of my favorite cooks helped to get this book into print: Charlotte Collins and Courtney Wade. Charlotte's passion is health and fitness and she has contributed her knowledge of healthier ingredients, diet recommendations, and an eclectic, highly nutritious way of eating throughout the day. Courtney, who has previously published a cookbook, lends expertise in combining flavors to suit anyone's tastes, and has a talent for food styling and photography. And given that they are both decades younger than me, you're sure to find a lot of fresh ideas to make you happy! Their enthusiasm has been absolutely infectious; we especially enjoyed sampling all the many kinds of pancakes during our test sessions.

I grew up with an old, black, cast iron, wood fired, cook stove. No, I'm not really that old, but I *did* grow up on a dairy farm and, as my parents enjoyed country life, they made a point of protecting tradition. I experimented with making bread, pizza, and meat loaf in it as I learned to cook, but the food that was the easiest, most consistent and most appreciated were pancakes. Right from the get-go, it was clear to me that pancakes make people happy.

I babysat my neighbor's three children from the start of her 6am nursing shift until it was time for the school bus. They would help me with my morning chores of feeding calves and then we would get breakfast. There was no store-bought cereal in our house: breakfast of champions was, you guessed it, pancakes. Boy, did those kids love a hot breakfast! They loved me for it, and still talk about it to this day.

As the years went on, I took over the family farm, and started concentrating on our maple syrup. There's only one thing I've found that makes pancakes taste better than sharing them with small children…and that's maple syrup! We trucked our syrup all over New York and peddled our products at the Union Square Greenmarket in NYC. In 1995, we began serving pancakes at the farm on weekends to showcase our pure maple syrup and the pancake mixes marketed under our own name. Even as farms struggled economically, and the picturesque landscape of open space and red barns began to disappear, it became clear to us the only thing people wanted more than pancakes was a farm experience. We started serving farm-to-table breakfasts, never losing sight of two things: we are a farm producing wholesome food, and it's our responsibility to share it with the public.

At our farm, coffee is served in mugs we have collected from thrift stores or been given as gifts. Our favorites are usually promotional ones from organizations or businesses from all over the map. For Christmas a few years back, my sister gave me a nice, hefty, ivory colored mug to add to our collection. The design on the front was a stack of pancakes, and the lettering read "Pancakes Make People Happy". One of our favorite customers, who just so happens to be the publisher of this book, really took a liking to this mug…and the rest is history!

Even though my days are very full working on the farm, when asked if I would like to write a pancake cookbook how could I say no? That's when I enlisted Charlotte and Courtney to do the heavy lifting. One with a degree in Direct & Interactive Marketing and the other in Graphic Design, they have done outstanding work in the "test kitchen" and the photos are as delicious as the recipes!

— *Sharon Collins, Buck Hill Farm*

Pancakes 101:
How to Use This Book

We have tried to make a book which will entertain not only the experienced cook, but also someone just getting started. For those of you who eat exclusively, i.e. gluten free, dairy free, vegan, low carb, it includes an informative chart of substitutions, so if you encounter a recipe that includes an ingredient that is not on your list of approved foods, please refer to the section called "Easy Substitutions". It will assist you in tailoring any recipe to suit your needs.

As you are using this cookbook, keep an eye out for helpful tips on the level of difficulty. Easy recipes for beginners and more involved recipes for fearless chefs are marked accordingly. Every recipe will have a symbol that rates the degree of difficulty from 1–4. They earn their ratings either because technique is very important to achieve the desired outcome, or because there are many ingredients and preparation is more challenging. Making pancakes is equal parts art and science. There are countless ways to artfully embellish your creations with your own personality, but for the moment let's go over some of the techniques that will guarantee the results you are looking for.

Use a heavy bottomed non-stick fry pan, an electric griddle with a thermostat, or a cast iron griddle. All work equally well. You will also need a reasonably large spatula for foolproof flipping. Try to find one that has a larger round end and isn't too flexible. Many recipes are very specific about cooking temperatures. For most, the griddle or stove should be set for 375°, or medium high. The griddle will be ready when a drop of water dances on it, or it begins to smoke after lightly greasing with vegetable oil or non-stick spray. Be patient while it heats. The most common mistake is pouring batter on a griddle that is either too hot or too cold. I suggest avoiding butter for greasing your cooking surface because it tends to burn at higher temperatures. You will need to grease your pan before pouring each batch of cakes and only lightly grease for proper browning (I like to wipe off excess oil with a paper towel each time). Frequently, the first pancake is destined for the family pet and you probably won't see perfection until the pan is well seasoned and evenly heated.

For best results, don't over-mix the batter and let it sit 5 to 10 minutes before cooking so the leavening process can start and the dry ingredients fully absorb the wet ingredients.

Make sure your batter is at room temperature. Cold batter will cool your cooking surface and result in a "tough" textured cake.

Do not peek at the underside of the pancake while it's cooking. Let it cook for two or three minutes on the first side (or as the recipe indicates) until the face of the pancake is covered with bubbles and the edges look dry. Then go ahead and flip it. Continue to cook two or three minutes more.

Don't forget, when it comes to pancakes, practice does make perfect.

Have fun and good luck!

Easy Substitutions

As you are planning your pancake party, be aware of your audience; our cookbook contains recipes for individuals with special health or diet requirements as well as tips for substituting or eliminating ingredients to suit their needs. Below is a list of common substitutions that will help convert any recipe to KETO, vegan, gluten-free, vegetarian, and/or dairy-free. Beware of substituting gluten free flours such as buckwheat or almond flour for all-purpose flour, as they generally do not behave the same way in baking. Knowing this, we have tried to include in our chapters numerous opportunities to use delicious gluten free and whole grain flours.

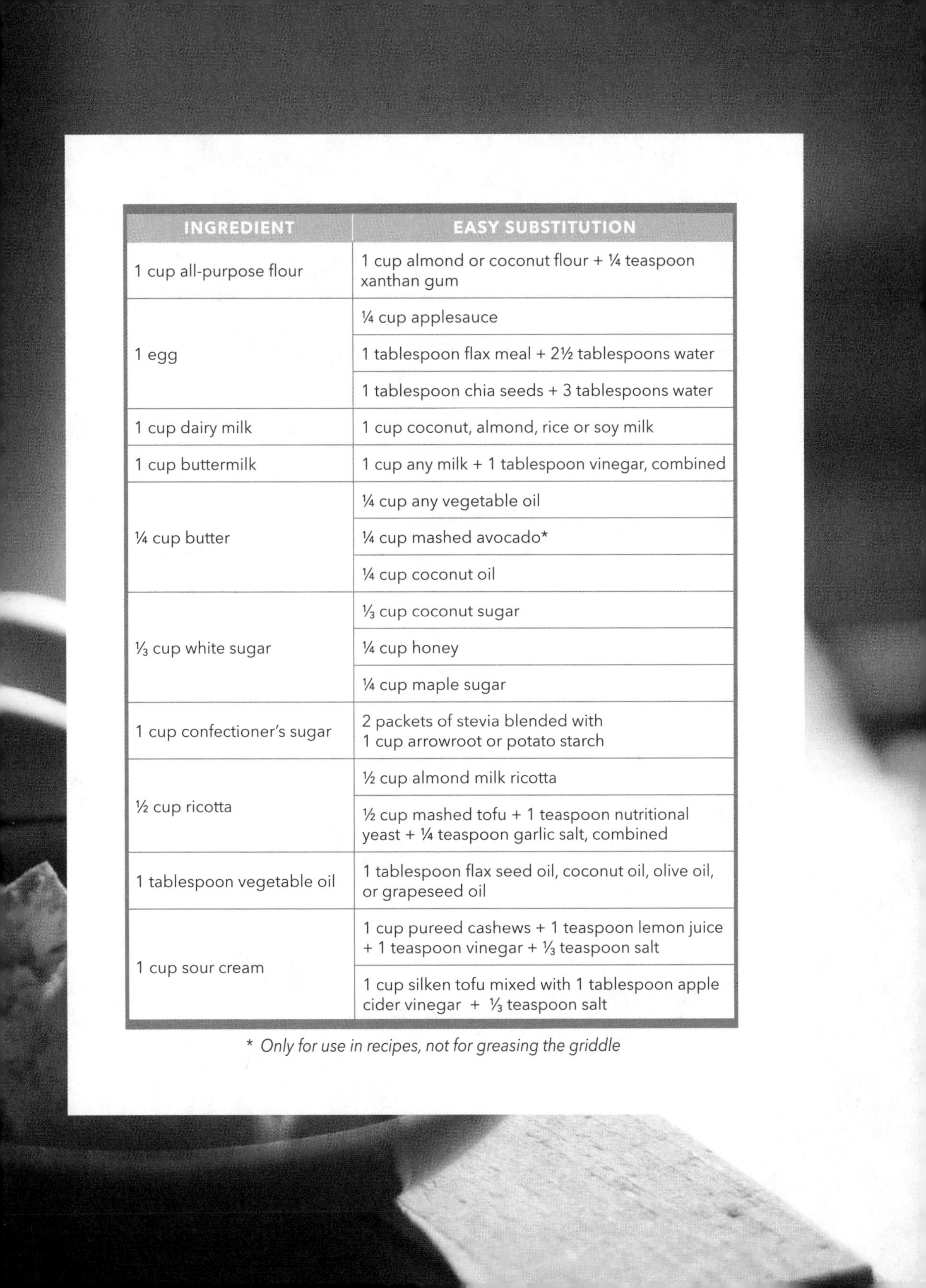

INGREDIENT	EASY SUBSTITUTION
1 cup all-purpose flour	1 cup almond or coconut flour + ¼ teaspoon xanthan gum
1 egg	¼ cup applesauce
	1 tablespoon flax meal + 2½ tablespoons water
	1 tablespoon chia seeds + 3 tablespoons water
1 cup dairy milk	1 cup coconut, almond, rice or soy milk
1 cup buttermilk	1 cup any milk + 1 tablespoon vinegar, combined
¼ cup butter	¼ cup any vegetable oil
	¼ cup mashed avocado*
	¼ cup coconut oil
⅓ cup white sugar	⅓ cup coconut sugar
	¼ cup honey
	¼ cup maple sugar
1 cup confectioner's sugar	2 packets of stevia blended with 1 cup arrowroot or potato starch
½ cup ricotta	½ cup almond milk ricotta
	½ cup mashed tofu + 1 teaspoon nutritional yeast + ¼ teaspoon garlic salt, combined
1 tablespoon vegetable oil	1 tablespoon flax seed oil, coconut oil, olive oil, or grapeseed oil
1 cup sour cream	1 cup pureed cashews + 1 teaspoon lemon juice + 1 teaspoon vinegar + ⅓ teaspoon salt
	1 cup silken tofu mixed with 1 tablespoon apple cider vinegar + ⅓ teaspoon salt

Only for use in recipes, not for greasing the griddle

The Recipes

Classic Pancakes

Pancakes themselves could be considered a "classic" food. So, it should be no surprise that one of the most popular pancake mix flavors on the market is called "Old Fashioned." We've decided to broaden this first chapter, and the meaning of classic, to include not only the go-to's for pancake batter, but flavor combinations and ingredients that seem to be timeless in the kitchen.

Old Fashioned Buttermilk Pancakes

DIFFICULTY: 1

Buttermilk pancakes are as classic as it gets. Made for over 30,000 years, pancakes have been found in the stomach of men frozen in the last ice age. They were also very popular with ancient Greeks and Romans, and most traditionally made with a flour and curdled milk, or as we call it today, buttermilk.

1½ cups milk

¼ cup white vinegar

2 cups flour

⅓ cup sugar

3 teaspoons baking powder

1 teaspoon baking soda

1 teaspoon salt

2 large eggs

1 teaspoon vanilla extract

¼ cup butter, melted, plus 1 tablespoon to grease the pan

1 tablespoon vegetable oil

Maple syrup or pancake syrup and butter, to serve

In a small bowl or measuring cup, combine milk and vinegar. Let sit for 10 minutes, or until the milk has curdled.

In the meantime, whisk the flour, sugar, baking powder, baking soda, and salt in a large bowl.

In a medium-sized bowl, combine the soured milk, eggs, ¼ cup of melted butter, and vanilla extract.

Pour the wet ingredients into the bowl of dry ingredients and stir until just combined. Remember, lumps are okay! Let the batter rest, undisturbed, for at least 5 minutes.

Melt remaining tablespoon of butter and tablespoon oil in a skillet over medium heat.

Pour ¼ cup of batter into your pan and use a rubber spatula to help even out.

Cook until the top fills with air bubbles, about 2½–3 minutes, then flip to cook the remaining side until cooked through and golden, about 1–2 minutes more. Remove the pancake from heat and place it on a plate. If you're finding that the outsides of your pancakes are cooking too quickly, reduce the heat accordingly. Continue until all pancakes are cooked.

Serve immediately with syrup and butter or let cool and freeze.

Buckwheat Pancakes

DIFFICULTY: 1
GLUTEN-FREE

We included buckwheat cakes in our classic chapter because for centuries buckwheat was a common flour. Buckwheat is very hearty and tends to grow like a weed, making it cheap and easily accessible. In contrast, white flour is the dusty by-product of milling grains and was only available in limited quantities. White flour makes lighter and more delicate cakes and breads and was usually reserved for the elite. If you ask around amidst your elderly relatives, you will probably hear at least one buckwheat batter story and recollections of its wholesome, nutty flavor. Despite the name, buckwheat is made from a seed, not a grain, which makes it an excellent option for the gluten-free eater.

½ cup buckwheat flour

½ cup unbleached flour (can substitute with gluten-free flour or rice flour)

2 eggs

⅔ cup milk (sub for dairy free)

1 tablespoon vegetable oil

2 teaspoons sugar

2 teaspoons baking powder

¼ teaspoons salt

In a medium bowl, combine dry ingredients. In a separate bowl, whisk together eggs, oil and milk. Add wet ingredients to dry ingredients. Heat skillet to medium, brush with vegetable oil. Pour batter and cook for 2 minutes until bubbles form, then flip and continue to cook for 2 minutes.

Leftover Herbed Smashed Potato Pancakes

DIFFICULTY: 2

The best potato cakes are made from leftover mashed potatoes (skins and all). You can also simply boil a few whole potatoes, let cool, and smash them up for equally delicious cakes.

PANCAKES

1½ cups Smashed
   potatoes

¼ cup flour

1 egg beaten

1 tablespoon chive

1 tablespoon parsley

½ teaspoon salt

¼ teaspoon pepper

Chopped scallions for
   garnish (optional)

Sour cream or yogurt
   for topping

CARAMELIZED ONIONS

1 large onion

1 tablespoon olive oil

1 tablespoon butter

1 teaspoon balsamic
   vinegar

½ teaspoon sugar

¼ teaspoon salt

Start by thinly slicing onion side to side into medallions. Heat a skillet with olive oil and butter. Throw all onions into the pan, coating evenly. After the onions begin to wilt, add remaining ingredients, stirring occasionally until caramelized (sticky and golden brown, about 10–15 minutes).

While the onions are cooking, mix all pancake ingredients together until creamy and well combined. Heat skillet on medium and rub the pan with butter until greased.

Form cakes with your hands into desired size (we made appetizer size), cooking 3 minutes per side or until well browned.

Dollop with sour cream or Greek yogurt, and garnish with caramelized onions and chopped scallions.

Fluffy Lemon Ricotta Pancakes

DIFFICULTY: 1

Lemon juice and ricotta cheese have been used in combination to add flavor and moistness to recipes since the beginning of time. For best results, use fresh squeezed lemon juice and whole milk ricotta cheese.

PANCAKES

1 cup flour

½ teaspoon baking powder

½ teaspoon baking soda

¼ teaspoon salt

2 tablespoons granulated sugar

¾ cup ricotta cheese

⅓ cup milk

1 large egg

1 teaspoon vanilla extract

1 tablespoon lemon juice

WHIPPED RICOTTA TOPPING

¾ cup ricotta

1 tablespoon powdered sugar

1 teaspoon vanilla extract

In a small mixing bowl whisk together flour, baking powder, baking soda, salt and sugar. In a medium mixing bowl combine ricotta cheese, milk, egg, vanilla and lemon juice. Whisk until smooth. Add the flour mixture to the ricotta mixture and stir together with a spatula. Set aside.

In a medium bowl using an electric mixer, whip together the ricotta, powdered sugar and vanilla, set aside.

Preheat a large non-stick skillet over medium heat. Lightly grease the pan with vegetable oil using a paper towel to remove the excess. Lower the heat to medium-low and add ¼ cup of batter for each pancake. Spread batter to desired size and thickness using a spoon or spatula. Cook until the bottom is golden brown and the edges are drying. Gently turn and continue cooking until browned and cooked through. Top with whipped ricotta topping and serve.

Peanut Butter Pancakes with Four Berry Compote

DIFFICULTY: 2

Don't be deterred by the long name—this is PB&J in pancake form, slightly elevated. We decided to designate the peanut butter flavor to the pancakes, and the jelly flavor for the topping. The best textures come from chunky peanut butter, and a whole berry homemade compote. We happened to have four kinds of berries on hand, and just like mixed berry pie, the more berry flavors the better, but use what you have!

PANCAKES

1½ cups flour

3½ teaspoons baking powder

¼ teaspoon baking soda

1 teaspoon salt

⅓ cup peanut butter

1 tablespoon distilled vinegar

1¼ cups milk

3 tablespoons maple syrup

1 teaspoon vanilla extract

1 egg

Butter or nonstick spray for greasing griddle

COMPOTE

1 cup mixed fruit (we used blueberry, blackberry, strawberry, raspberry)

⅓ cup sugar

In a small bowl, mix together vinegar and milk of your choice. Let sit while preparing dry ingredients.

Whisk together flour, baking soda, baking powder and salt.

Add peanut butter, egg, and vanilla to milk mixture and mix until incorporated. Add this mixture to dry ingredients and milk until just combined. Add a little extra milk if the batter is still too thick. Set aside.

Combine fruit and sugar in a small saucepan over medium-high heat. Cook until thickened and fruit is broken down (about 5–7 min).

Preheat a griddle or non-stick pan over medium heat. Spray or grease. Once pan is heated, dollop about ¼ cup of batter onto the griddle. Cook pancakes until bubbles form on top of surface and then carefully flip. Cook for another 1–2 minutes and remove. Serve with berry compote.

Cornmeal Cakes

DIFFICULTY: 1

Cornmeal Cakes, Johnny Cakes, Journey Cakes, Spider Cornbread, Hoe Cake, Shawnee Cake…they're all names given to a pancake made out of cornmeal. This one earned its place in our Classic chapter because the first cornmeal cakes were made from a corn called maize grown by indigenous people of North America. It went on to become a staple food for generations of early Americans.

¾ cup flour

¾ cup yellow cornmeal

2 tablespoons sugar

½ teaspoon baking powder

½ teaspoon baking soda

½ teaspoon salt

1¼ cups buttermilk (or 1¼ cups milk + 1 generous tablespoons vinegar)

2 large eggs

3 tablespoons butter, melted

Oil or butter for greasing

Mix the first six ingredients in a large bowl. If you don't have buttermilk, combine the milk and vinegar and let sit for 5 minutes. Whisk buttermilk, eggs and melted butter in a medium bowl. Add buttermilk mixture to dry ingredients and whisk until smooth.

Heat griddle to medium heat. Grease your griddle (or pan) and pour ¼ cup batter for each pancake. Cook until bottoms are golden, about 1–2 minutes. Turn pancakes and cook until the second side turns up golden, about 1 minute.

Pancakes Make People Happy

Banana Bread Pancakes with Caramelized Bananas

DIFFICULTY: 2

Pancakes with fruit need no explanation. Bananas are second only to blueberries in popularity amongst pancake fans. This classic recipe steps it up a notch with caramelized bananas. It's a great way to use up very ripe bananas and the depth of flavor is astounding.

PANCAKES

1 cup flour

1 tablespoon sugar

1 tablespoon brown sugar

2 teaspoons baking powder

¼ teaspoon salt

1 egg

1 cup milk

2 tablespoons butter, melted

½ teaspoon vanilla

2 medium very ripe bananas, mashed

⅓ cup roughly chopped walnuts

CARAMELIZED BANANAS

1 banana, sliced into coins

¼ cup brown sugar

2 tablespoons butter

Preheat a skillet, pan, or griddle to medium heat. In a medium bowl whisk together flour, sugar, brown sugar, baking powder, and salt. In another bowl mix together egg, milk, butter, vanilla, and mashed bananas. Add dry ingredients to wet ingredients and mix until just combined (do not overmix). Gently stir in nuts.

Lightly grease your preheated skillet. Pour ¼ cup batter onto the skillet. Cook for 1–2 minutes, until the edges begin to look "dry". Flip with spatula, cook another 1–2 minutes. Repeat with remaining batter.

Bananas

Melt butter in a pan over medium heat. Add brown sugar and stir to combine. Add banana slices and stir to coat, cooking until browned on each side and brown sugar has clumped (about 5 minutes total). Arrange bananas atop finished pancakes and serve.

Hardy Polenta Cakes

DIFFICULTY: 1

Polenta is a very thick porridge with a slightly grainy texture. Sliced and fried, it's pancakes classic Italian style. We used ready to cook dry grits for this recipe, but you can also purchase premade polenta in a tube. Usually found in the produce section of the supermarket.

2 cups Corn Polenta Grits

2 tablespoons butter

Powdered sugar and favorite fresh berries for topping

Cook your polenta grits with 6 quarts water, or according to package directions. If using premade polenta, slice your polenta in ¼–½-inch rounds.

Heat a skillet over medium heat, once hot add a pat of butter. Add polenta rounds, cook for 2 minutes per side or until lightly golden and crisp on the edges. Remove from the pan, place on a plate. Repeat with the remaining polenta.

Serve with a sprinkle of powdered sugar, fresh fruit, and more butter if you please.

Sour Cream Pancakes

DIFFICULTY: 1

Here's another classic pancake, particularly popular on Fat Tuesday or Shrove Tuesday. Fat Tuesday is the Tuesday before Ash Wednesday (and supposedly 40 days before Easter), when Christians historically ate up all the rich and fatty foods (dairy, eggs, and meats or in other words, foods that would spoil) in their household before beginning their ritual fast for the Lenten season.

1 shy cup flour

1 tablespoon sugar

1 teaspoon baking soda

½ teaspoon salt

1 cup sour cream

2 large eggs

½ teaspoon almond extract

Slivered almonds (for topping)

Jam or compote (for topping)

Butter for greasing

Heat a skillet or griddle over medium heat. Mix the flour, sugar, baking soda and salt together in a medium bowl. Gently stir in sour cream.

Whisk the eggs and almond extract in a separate bowl and stir them into the sour cream mixture, once again, being careful not to overmix.

Melt butter in your skillet or griddle and pour the batter in, a scant ¼ cup at a time. Cook for about 2 minutes on the first side, or until bubbles appear all over the surface, flipping and cooking for another minute. Repeat with remaining batter.

Serve topped with jam and almonds.

Einkorn Cakes

DIFFICULTY: 1

Einkorn is an ancient grain, and one of the first grains to be domesticated around 7,500 B.C. in the Middle Eastern region of Central Europe. Packed with fiber and protein it deserves a place on the classic list.

1½ cups Einkorn Flour

1 tablespoon baking powder

¼ teaspoon salt

2 large eggs

1 cup almond milk

4 tablespoons coconut oil melted, plus more for greasing skillet

½ teaspoon vanilla

2 tablespoons raw honey

Whisk to combine the eggs, honey, vanilla, and milk. Stir together the einkorn flour, baking powder, and salt into a medium bowl.

Add the dry ingredients into the egg/milk mixture. Stir until just combined.

Add in the melted coconut oil and mix into the batter.

Preheat a griddle or skillet. Grease the skillet with oil or butter. Use a ¼ measuring cup to pour the batter onto the skillet. Cook until the batter begins to bubble and then flip to the other side. Cook time is approximately 2–3 minutes on each side.

Savory Pancakes

By and large, pancakes are usually served up sweet with sticky syrup or fruit toppings, but we are hoping to expand your palette with a whole chapter of savory options. For us, this was a most exciting adventure! Pancakes are very versatile food vehicles, inviting all kinds of interesting ingredients and flavors.

White Cheddar Zucchini Cakes with Honey & Rosemary

DIFFICULTY: 2

These savory pancakes are incredibly versatile. They can be made tiny to pass as hors d'oeuvres at a party, small for a tapas plate, or larger for a main course. This recipe earns it difficulty level 2 only because it's a bit of a chore to grate the zucchini and then squeeze the excess water out of it—but pain though it may be, it is oh-so-important to success!

2 cups grated zucchini (squeezed and drained in a colander before measuring)

½ cup all-purpose flour

½ cup grated white cheddar

2 eggs

2 tablespoons rosemary

½ teaspoon salt

½ teaspoon pepper

Olive oil (for frying)

Begin by thoroughly draining grated zucchini of any excess water, squeezing with your hands and draining through a colander. Beat eggs, then add your grated zucchini, flour, grated cheddar, herbs and spices.

Heat a skillet on medium-low, drizzling and spreading around 1–2 tablespoons of olive oil. Spoon the batter into the skillet forming 4-inch cakes. Cook 3–4 minutes each side or until brown and crispy.

Jalapeño Corn Fritter Pancakes

DIFFICULTY: 1

These Jalapeno Fritter Cakes make a great side for breakfast or dinner. Try them with fried chicken or as a foundation for eggs benedict.

½ cup water

½ cup corn

1 teaspoon minced jalapeno (depending on spiciness)

½ teaspoon salt

1 tablespoon olive oil

Mix together flour and water until combined. Stir in corn, jalapeno and salt.

Heat a skillet to medium. Scoop batter from the bottom of the bowl as the corn tends to sink as it sits. Cook pancakes 2–3 minutes on each side, or until browned.

Cabbage Pancakes

DIFFICULTY: 2

These are a crunchy, fiber-filled, savory favorite of ours, and you can get almost anyone to eat their veggies in pancake form! This recipe is flexible as well. If you don't happen to have every ingredient, substitute any root vegetable for the carrot, or toss in kale and onion instead of green onion. It's hard to go wrong here.

PANCAKES

2 eggs

½ cup water

2 tablespoons soy sauce

1 tablespoon olive oil

¾–1 cup flour

4–5 cups shredded green
  cabbage

1 carrot

3 green onions

2 tablespoons oil for
  frying

SAUCE

¼ cup mayo

2 tablespoons sriracha

Remove outer leaves from cabbage. Cut into quarters and remove the core. Thinly slice or shred half the cabbage until you have 4–5 cups. Peel the carrot and grate it using a cheese grater. Slice the green onions.

In a large bowl, whisk the eggs, water, soy sauce and oil until smooth. Whisk in the flour ¼ cup at a time, until it forms a smooth, thick batter, using up to 1 cup if needed.

Add the cabbage, carrot, and green onion to the batter and stir until the veggies are combined and everything is evenly coated in batter.

Heat ½ tablespoon of oil on a griddle or skillet over medium heat. When heated, add ¾ cup of the mixture. Press it down on the hot skillet to form about a 6-inch circle, ½-inch thick. Place a cover over the pancake to steam. Cook until golden brown, about 3–5 minutes, then flip and cook until golden on the other side. To keep cooked pancakes warm, place them on a plate and cover with foil. Add more oil to the pan as needed.

To make sauce, mix together mayo and sriracha in a small bowl. Drizzle sriracha mayo over the prepared pancakes just before serving. Sprinkle with extra green onion.

Crispy Risotto Pancake

DIFFICULTY: 1

We're big fans of using up leftovers to avoid waste. We're also determined that almost any ingredient can be included in a pancake recipe. This recipe is how leftover risotto becomes a risotto pancake. Incredibly delicious and easy, and we will reserve all judgement if you make fresh risotto just to make this pancake.

2½ tablespoons butter

2 cups leftover risotto, fully cooled

Grated parmesan cheese

Melt butter over high heat in a 10-inch non-stick skillet. Add risotto, and using a spatula, pat it down to form into a round pancake shape.

Continue cooking over high heat, patting the top and sides to keep its shape. Swirl the pan to prevent the pancake from sticking and cook until very well browned on the bottom. The edges will be browned, indicating that it is ready to flip. If the pancake comes apart as you swirl it, use the spatula to press it back together.

With a large spatula, in one very quick motion, flip the pancake. Use spatula to patch any spots that were damaged during flipping. Continue cooking, swirling, and patting with spatula until the second side is well browned.

Carefully slide the pancake onto a warmed serving plate and top with freshly grated cheese. Serve immediately.

Buckwheat Galettes

DIFFICULTY: 2
GLUTEN-FREE, VEGAN

A galette is another term for a crusty, free form cake. (You say cake, we say pancake, right?) Buckwheat flour and savory fillings are common for galettes, so we've adapted a folded crepe-like cake and stuffed it with a good old egg-veggie-cheese combo. You've got this!

1½ cups buckwheat
pancake mix*

1½ teaspoons salt

1 egg

1¼ cups whole milk

1⅓ cups water

Fried eggs

Sautéed mushrooms

Shredded cheese

* We used Buck Hill Farm
buckwheat pancake mix,
but you can also follow our
Buckwheat pancake recipe in
the Classic chapter.

In a large bowl, whisk together buckwheat pancake flour, and salt. Add egg, milk, and water and whisk until thoroughly combined. Let batter stand for about 10 minutes, or until bubbles begin to form.

In a nonstick skillet, melt about ½ tablespoon butter over high heat until browned and starting to smoke. Add ⅓ cup of batter to the pan, swirling to evenly cover. Return to heat and let cook until the bottom is beginning to brown well and the top looks dry, 30 seconds to 1 minute. Reduce heat at any point to prevent burning.

To fill crepes, start by spreading a small handful of grated cheese around the center of the crepe while it's still in the pan, on the heat. Spoon sautéed mushrooms over cheese and place a fried egg over top. Using a thin metal spatula, fold sides of crepe in to form a rectangular shape with egg yolk exposed. Continue to cook until the bottom is well browned and crisp, about 30 seconds. Serve, then repeat with remaining crepe batter, butter, and fillings.

To Make Crepes for Another Purpose

Carefully free crepe from pan with a thin metal spatula, then flip and cook the other side for about 10 seconds. Transfer to a plate. Continue with remaining crepe batter and butter. Keep cooked crepes stacked and covered with a clean kitchen towel while cooking remaining crepes. Crepes can be held for about 1 hour before using, then quickly reheated in a skillet.

Whipped Saffron & Pea Cakes

DIFFICULTY: 3

Saffron is the most expensive spice in the world by weight. It makes a great gift for the chef in the family. We recognize that this fact makes it unlikely to be a staple in the common kitchen. But if you do have it on hand, it adds incredible color and aroma. This recipe comes in a few steps making it a bit more laborious, but delivers a light, elevated pancake to impress friends or family.

1 large clove garlic, minced

2 tablespoons olive oil

⅛ teaspoon loosely packed saffron threads*

½ teaspoon turmeric (can substitute curry powder for additional flavor)

1 cup shelled peas

8 ounces whole milk ricotta

2 large eggs, separated

¼ teaspoon salt

¼ cup freshly grated Parmesan

¼ cup spelt flour

1-2 tablespoons chopped chives (optional)

Heat a griddle or skillet over medium heat and coat with olive oil. Add the garlic, and crumble in the saffron threads. Cook, stirring frequently, until fragrant. Be careful not to burn.

Add the peas and cook for 1–2 minutes. Remove from the heat and set aside.

Combine the ricotta, turmeric, egg yolks (save the egg whites), salt, parmesan, and spelt flour to a large bowl and stir to combine. Gently stir in the garlic/pea mixture until combined.

In a medium bowl, use an electric mixer to whip the egg whites until they hold soft peaks. Stir ⅓ of the whipped whites into the batter to loosen it up, then gently fold in the remaining egg whites until just combined.

Heat the same skillet over medium heat and coat with olive oil. When the oil shimmers, drop two or three ¼-cup scoops of batter into the pan. Cook until the first side is golden, 2–3 minutes, then flip and cook on the second side until golden and cooked through, about 2 minutes. Remove to a platter. Serve the cakes topped with salt, pepper and chives.

* You can substitute saffron with ½ teaspoon curry powder or a simpler spice like garlic powder.

Basil Orange Ricotta Cakes

DIFFICULTY: 1

Basil pairs incredibly well with citrus flavors. We find these to have the perfect combination of taste and texture. Fresh basil is imperative.

1½ cups flour

1 teaspoon baking powder

¼ teaspoon salt

Zest of ½ orange

3 tablespoons chopped fresh basil

1 egg

½ cup whole milk ricotta

Juice of ½ an orange

2 tablespoons maple syrup

3 tablespoons butter, melted

¾ cup whole milk

Combine flour, baking powder and salt in a large bowl. Whisk together all remaining ingredients in a small bowl. Pour the wet ingredients into the dry and mix together. Heat a skillet or griddle over medium heat and grease or spray with oil. Spoon batter onto the griddle (you may have to spread into a circle with the back of a spoon) and cook for 1–2 minutes per side. Serve with a sprinkle of salt.

Spinach Pancakes

DIFFICULTY: 1

This was our take on a spinach salad, but obviously in pancake form. The pancakes take away any aversions one might have to spinach, such as texture or bitterness, and offer an incredibly easy way to add some greens to your diet. Really, these pancakes are GREEN.

1 cup packed fresh spinach

1 cup buttermilk

1 egg

1 tablespoon oil

1 cup flour

1 tablespoon sugar

1 teaspoon baking powder

½ teaspoon baking soda

½ teaspoon salt

Walnuts, fresh strawberries, balsamic glaze (optional)

In a blender, combine the spinach, buttermilk, egg, and oil and blend until smooth. In a separate bowl, whisk together the remaining ingredients. Whisk the wet ingredients into the dry ingredients until just combined.

Heat a large pan or griddle over medium heat and grease with butter or oil. Pour ⅓ cup batter onto the griddle and cook until bubbles form, then flip. Continue cooking until edges are fully cooked, about 2 minutes.

This recipe works great as is for a standard waffle maker! These pancakes are also very low in sugar and can easily be made with whole wheat flour for a heart-healthier option.

Chickpea Pancakes with Broccoli Rabe & Roasted Chickpeas

DIFFICULTY: 4

This recipe is designated Difficulty 4 because there are quite a few steps in the cooking process as well some extra ingredients. You will also have to use both the stove top and oven, but it will be well worth it. These savory pancakes are a showstopper!

PANCAKES

½ cup chickpea flour

½ cup water

1 tablespoon olive oil

Salt

ROASTED CHICKPEAS

1 (15 ounce) can chickpeas, drained and rinsed

2 tablespoons olive oil

½ teaspoon toasted fennel seeds

½ teaspoon chili pepper flakes

½ teaspoon chili powder

½ teaspoon salt

½ teaspoon black pepper

½ teaspoon garlic powder

1 large garlic clove, crushed

TAHINI SAUCE

¼ cup tahini

1 tablespoon olive oil

1 tablespoon water

1 tablespoon fresh lemon juice

1 clove garlic

1 tablespoon olive oil

½ bunch broccoli rabe

Salt and pepper

Garlic powder

To make pancake batter, combine flour, water, olive oil, and a pinch of salt in a medium bowl. Whisk until smooth and let batter stand for 10 minutes.

Preheat the oven to 375°F. Combine all roasted chickpea ingredients in a medium bowl and toss until coated. Place chickpeas on a baking sheet and bake for 15 minutes.

To make sauce, combine tahini, olive oil and lemon juice in a small bowl. Finely grate garlic clove and mix to combine sauce. If the sauce is too thick, add up to a tablespoon of water.

Heat olive oil over medium heat in a medium skillet. Roughly chop broccoli rabe and discard the lower stems. Add to the heated pan and cook until wilted and dark green in color, about 5 minutes. Season with salt, pepper, and garlic powder to taste.

To cook pancakes, heat a griddle coated with nonstick spray on high heat. Slowly pour ¼ cup of batter for each pancake on the griddle. Batter will be very thin and will spread. Cook pancakes until golden brown, about 2–3 minutes. Flip and cook the second side until browned, about a minute more. Transfer to a plate, and continue with remaining batter. Top pancakes with Sautéed broccoli, roasted chickpeas and tahini sauce, and serve.

Pistachio Pancakes
with Pistachio Chevre

DIFFICULTY: 2

If you're a pistachio nut, bookmark this page. We toss pistachios *in* the pancakes, grind them into creamy cheese topping, and throw some more on top. Goat cheese has its own natural saltiness, but you can amplify the depth of flavor by using salted pistachios.

1½ cups flour

⅓ cup + 3 tablespoons separated finely ground pistachios

2 tablespoons sugar

1 teaspoon baking powder

1 teaspoon baking soda

¼ teaspoon salt

2 eggs

1¼ cups milk

1 teaspoon vanilla

2 tablespoons butter

4 ounces chevre goat cheese*

* *Goat cheese and chevre are the same thing, for shopping reference. Be sure to buy shelled pistachios (unless you've got some time to kill shelling them yourself!).*

In a large bowl, combine the flour, pistachios, sugar, baking powder, soda and salt. In a smaller bowl, whisk together the eggs, milk, vanilla and butter. Add the wet ingredients to the dry, mixing until smooth.

Let batter sit while creaming together 3 tablespoons of reserved pistachios and goat cheese together in a small food processor or with an electric mixer.

Heat a large skillet or griddle over medium heat. Add a bit of butter to grease, then pour ¼ cup of batter on the hot skillet. Cook until the pancakes bubble on the top and edges, about 2 minutes. Flip and cook for another minute or two until golden and set. Top with a smear of pistachio chevre.

Kimchi Pancakes

DIFFICULTY: 1

There are usually three levels of Kimchi awareness: you either love it and always have it in the fridge, hate it and can't understand its popularity, or have never heard of it. For all of you, this is a chance to embrace it in the familiar form of a pancake.

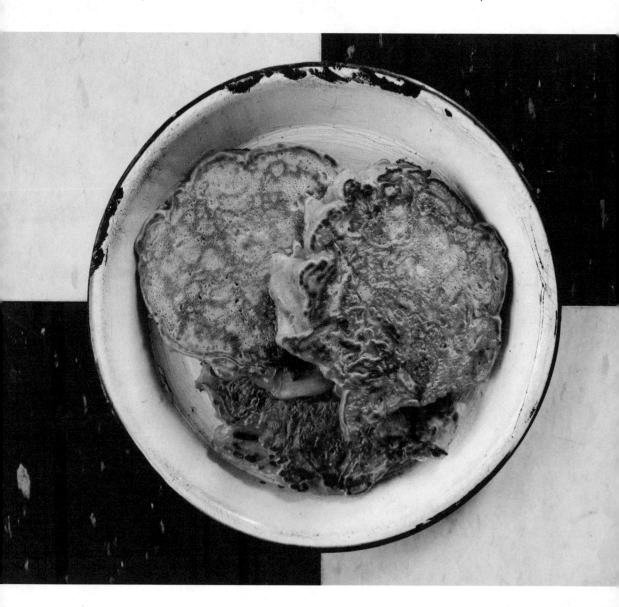

1 egg

1 tablespoon kimchi
  brine from jar

¼ cup soy sauce

¼ cup water

¾ cup + 1 tablespoon
  flour

1½ cups kimchi

3 tablespoons white
  vinegar

Oil, for cooking

Crack 1 egg into a medium bowl. Add 1 tablespoon kimchi brine, 1 tablespoon soy sauce, and ¼ cup water and whisk to combine. Whisk in flour.

Coarsely chop 1½ cups kimchi, add to bowl, and stir to combine.

Heat oil in a medium skillet over medium-high. Drop ¼-cupfulls of batter about 4 inches in diameter. Cook pancakes until golden brown on first side, 2–3 minutes, then flip and cook until browned on the second side, 2–3 minutes longer. Transfer to a wire rack and let cool.

Repeat process in batches. Combine vinegar and remaining soy sauce in a small bowl for dipping.

Squash & Eggplant Pancakes with Pickled Red Onions

DIFFICULTY: 4

We say these are difficult because they do take time, but you don't need a culinary degree to find each step very manageable. We have included each ingredient because it will result in the perfect savory flavor explosion. Acidic pickled onions, creamy tzatziki and freshly grated vegetable herb pancakes. Give them a try.

PICKLED RED ONIONS

1 medium red onion, thinly sliced

1 cup cider vinegar

2 bay leaves

1 teaspoon salt

½ teaspoon peppercorns

½ teaspoon coriander

SOUR CREAM TZATZIKI

½ cup sour cream

Juice from ½ a lemon

½ cup finely chopped fresh mint

1 mini cucumber, peeled and finely diced

Salt

Pepper

Arugula* (for topping)

PANCAKES

2 cups grated eggplant*, skin on

2 cups grated yellow squash or zucchini*

Juice from ½ lemon

½ cup fresh spinach, chopped

1 tablespoon fresh mint, finely chopped

3 eggs, beaten

1 cup flour

¼ cup freshly grated parmesan cheese

Salt

Pepper

To make the pickled red onions, combine the vinegar, bay leaves, peppercorns, coriander and salt in a medium saucepan and bring to a boil. Meanwhile, cram sliced onions into a quart mason jar. Pour hot liquid over onions and let bring to room temperature. When cooled, cover and refrigerate until ready to use. May be stored for up to two weeks.

To make tzatziki sauce, combine all ingredients in a small bowl and mix to combine. Season with salt and pepper to taste.

For pancakes, place grated eggplant and grated squash in a clean towel and squeeze out liquid. Place veggies in a large bowl and squeeze lemon juice over the mixture to prevent browning of the eggplant. Add chopped spinach, mint, beaten eggs, flour and parmesan. Let the mixture stand for 30 minutes.

If there is any excess liquid in the bottom of the bowl after the 30 minutes, carefully pour out. Season with the desired amount of salt and pepper.

Heat griddle to medium high heat and grease with olive oil. Take a ¼–⅓ cup of batter and form a pancake on the hot griddle. Cook until the bottom is golden brown. Flip and cook until the second side is golden and center is cooked through, about 6 minutes total. Continue with remaining batter. Top pancakes with arugula, pickled red onions and tzatziki sauce.

* *Best attempted in summer when squash, eggplant and arugula are all in season.*

Brunch
Pancakes

This chapter includes recipes that are extra indulgent, appropriate for a group, and even possibly on the boozy side.

Brunchy Dutch Baby

DIFFICULTY: 2

It feels like 99 percent of the work that goes into a Dutch baby is in its presentation…
but that doesn't mean it's not worth it! We were actually gawking at the end result;
we couldn't *believe* how easy it was! There's magic happening in the oven, I swear.

¼ cup butter, plus additional butter for serving

6 large eggs, at room temperature

⅔ cup whole milk, at room temperature

⅔ cup all-purpose flour

½ teaspoon kosher salt

¼ teaspoon cracked pepper

¼ cup + 3 tablespoons grated parmesan cheese, divided

¼ cup grated gouda cheese (or your favorite melting cheese)

⅓ red onion, sliced

1 tablespoon fresh thyme leaves

1 tablespoon chopped fresh chives

Preheat the oven to 450°F. Place 2 tablespoons butter in a 10-inch cast iron skillet.

Place the skillet in the oven for 5 minutes.

Whisk together 4 eggs, milk, flour, salt, pepper, and 2 tablespoons melted butter until smooth.

In a small bowl, combine the parmesan, gouda, thyme, and chives.

Remove the hot skillet from the oven and pour the batter into the skillet. Quickly sprinkle the cheese/herb mix gently over top of the batter. Place the skillet in the center of the oven and bake for 20 minutes or until the pancake is fully puffed and but not quite done browning. DO NOT open the oven during the first 15 minutes of cooking or you might deflate your pancake.

Moving quickly, remove the skillet from the oven to crack 2 remaining eggs on the center of the pancake, topping with remaining 3 tablespoons parmesan and sliced onion. Return the skillet to the oven for a final 5 minutes of cooking, until browned and eggs are just set.

Remove the Dutch Baby from the oven and top with a small pat of butter. Finish with another pinch of cracked pepper.

Cranberry Rum Pancakes with Butter Rum Syrup

DIFFICULTY: 2

Rum is inherently sweet, making the perfect complement to tart cranberry flavor. The sauce really makes this recipe, so don't skip it!

PANCAKES

2 cups self-rising flour

2 eggs

2 tablespoons white sugar

1½ cups whole milk

½ cup dried cranberries

1 tablespoon rum

1 teaspoon vanilla extract

½ teaspoon cinnamon

Pinch of salt

1 tablespoon olive oil

Powdered sugar (optional topping)

RUM BUTTER SAUCE

4 tablespoons butter

1 tablespoon rum

2 tablespoons dried cranberries

⅓ cup pure maple syrup

Combine all ingredients in a large bowl, and whisk until smooth. Set aside to rest for 15 minutes.

To make the rum butter sauce, combine all ingredients in a small saucepan on low heat. Simmer until the butter has melted. Remove from the heat and leave in the pan to keep warm.

Heat a skillet on medium heat. Pour ½–⅓ cup pancake batter on the center of the hot pan and gently spread the batter to form a circle. Cook until bubbles appear on the surface.

Using a spatula, flip pancake over and cook the other side for a minute, or until golden. Repeat with remaining batter.

Serve pancakes drizzled with rum butter sauce. Sprinkle with powdered sugar if desired.

Crunchy Granola Pancakes with Blackberry Butter

DIFFICULTY: 2
GLUTEN-FREE

You can make anything indulgent with flavored butter, right? For those on a gluten free diet, these pancakes won't leave anything to be desired. Crunchy, sweet pancakes with fruity butter. If you have a favorite granola use it, any kind will work.

PANCAKES

½ cup milk

2 large eggs

1 large egg white

1 large ripe banana

2 tablespoons maple syrup

1½ cups rolled oats

½ cup coconut flour or almond meal (they add nice texture, but can also be substituted for regular flours)

2 teaspoons baking powder

½ teaspoon salt

1 teaspoon vanilla

1½ cups granola

BUTTER

½ cup salted butter

⅓ cup blackberries

Pour milk, eggs, egg white, banana, maple syrup, vanilla, rolled oats, coconut flour, baking powder and salt into a blender. Blend until smooth.

Whip butter and blackberries together until fluffy and combine (there will be seeds stuck around the bowl from the berries). Set aside.

Heat skillet over medium heat. Once warmed, spray with non-stick cooking spray or place coconut oil or butter in the skillet. Pour pancake batter into skillet in round circles.

Evenly sprinkle the top side with ¼ cup granola. Cook for 2–3 minutes on one side. Flip and cook for another 1–2 minutes. Top pancakes with more granola and dollop of blackberry butter.

Monte Cristo Pancakes

DIFFICULTY: 2

A Monte Cristo sandwich is a fried ham and cheese sandwich, a variation of the French croque-monsieur. We are taking our classic buttermilk pancakes here and making a fried sandwich with them. It's a deluxe ham and cheese sandwich made mysterious and elegant, sure to delight anyone sitting down to brunch.

PANCAKES

2 cups buttermilk mix (from our buttermilk recipe)

1 cup water

FILLING

4 slices gouda, or other melting cheese

4 slices ham thinly sliced

2 tablespoons strawberry jam (or preferred jam)

EGG WASH

2 eggs

½ cup milk

¼ teaspoon cinnamon

Heat pancake griddle to medium heat. Lightly grease griddle. Whisk together pancake mix and water. Batter will be slightly lumpy. (Do not overmix.) Let batter stand 2 minutes. Pour slightly less than ¼ cup batter per pancake onto griddle. You should make an equal number of pancakes to make sure you have complete sandwiches!

Cook pancakes 1–2 minutes per side or until golden.

Spread ½ tablespoon of jam on half of the pancakes. Top the jam with a slice of cheese and a slice of ham. Top with another pancake.

In a shallow bowl, whisk together the eggs, milk, and cinnamon. Carefully dip one pancake sandwich into the egg mixture, coating both sides. Place on the hot skillet and cook for 3 minutes on each side, or until the outsides are golden brown and the cheese is melted. To help the cheese melt, you can cover the whole sandwich with a large lid. Repeat with all pancakes. Serve warm, dusted with powdered sugar.

Bacon & Salted Honey Pancake

DIFFICULTY: 3

It wouldn't be a brunch chapter without bacon in there somewhere. If you are a fan of the salty, sweet combination, this recipe is for you. It's a level 3 because the cooking process is a bit tricky but well worth it. It's important to note that this recipe will make two thick, 8-inch skillet cakes, and it's plenty to share. The pancake can essentially be sliced like a frittata.

2-3 strips bacon

¼ teaspoon flaky sea salt

1¼ cup flour

1 tablespoon brown sugar

2½ teaspoons baking powder

1¼ cups whole milk

2 tablespoons canola oil

1 tablespoon water

2 tablespoons butter, melted

Honey or maple syrup, to serve

Mince the bacon into bits. In a small well-seasoned skillet, cook the minced bacon over medium heat for 4–5 min, until the fat is rendered and bits are crispy. Spoon bacon bits into a small bowl, holding the spoon to the side of the skillet to leave drippings behind. Toss bacon with salt and set aside.

Mix together flour, brown sugar, baking powder, whole milk, canola oil and water just until relatively smooth (small lumps are fine). Add enough melted butter to the skillet so you have about 2 tablespoons of fat in total (including bacon drippings) and set over medium heat.

Once the butter starts to bubble, pour in the batter, then gently tuck in the sides with a spatula to make the edges smooth. Put a lid on, then turn the heat down to medium/medium-low and cook for about 8–11 minutes. Try not to lift the lid in the first 8 min, or you'll lose steam and the pancake may not cook properly. After 8 min, check and see if a deeply caramelized and crispy bottom-crust has formed (it's ok if the center of the batter still looks a bit runny). If not, put the lid back on and cook for another couple min.

When it's ready to be flipped, I find it easier to gently lift the pancake with a fork, then insert a wide spatula underneath. Gently lift the pancake, then tilt the skillet slightly towards it and flip the pancake over. Pour another 1 tablespoon of melted butter along the edges and cook for another 4–5 min over medium-low heat until the other side is browned and crispy.

Serve the pancake immediately, with bacon bits and honey or maple syrup.

Avocado Pancakes

DIFFICULTY: 2

Avocado is an incredibly versatile ingredient that can be a great substitute for butter or oils because it adds creaminess and moisture. In these circumstances, avocado is a dairy free alternative that adds vitamins, minerals, and healthy fats to your recipe. Avocados are also a fruit, so they pair great with other fruits, hence our blueberry compote topper!

PANCAKES

1½ cups flour

1 tablespoon baking powder

1 teaspoon salt

1 avocado

1 teaspoon lime juice

3 tablespoons honey

1 teaspoon lime zest

1 cup + 2 tablespoons buttermilk

2 eggs

½ teaspoon vanilla

BLUEBERRY COMPOTE

1 cup blueberries

¼ cup sugar

½ teaspoon lime zest

In a large bowl, whisk together flour, baking powder, and salt. In a medium bowl, mash avocado and lime juice with a fork until smooth. Whisk in honey, zest, and buttermilk. Add eggs and vanilla and whisk until fully combined.

Add wet ingredients to dry ingredients and stir until just combined. In a large skillet over medium-low heat, melt a pat of butter. Ladle ⅓ cup of batter into skillet. Cook until bubbles start to form and the pancake is golden underneath, about 6 minutes. Flip and cook until the other side is golden, about 4 minutes. Repeat with remaining batter.

To make compote, combine berries, sugar and zest in a saucepan over medium heat. Cook until berries begin to burst and mixture begins to bubble. Serve pancakes with warm berry compote over top.

Citrus Mimosa Pancakes

DIFFICULTY: 1

Finally, light and refreshing pancakes! Mimosas are such a classic brunch food that we had to invent a pancake recipe to honor them. It might not be immediately obvious, but the fruity, yeasty, and sometimes nutty flavor of Champagne goes great in food. Top your pancakes with a beautiful color palette of citrus for an impressive table at your next brunch.

2 cups flour

2 teaspoons baking powder

½ teaspoon salt

½ cup milk

2 tablespoons sugar

1 teaspoon orange zest + ½ cup fresh orange juice

2 eggs

2 tablespoons oil

¼ cup sparkling wine or champagne

Powdered sugar, for topping

Orange and grapefruit chunks or slices, for topping

Whisk together flour, baking powder and salt. Make a well in the center of the bowl and add milk, sugar, orange zest and juice, eggs, oil and sparkling wine. Using a whisk, break up wet ingredients and incorporate into dry ingredients. Mix until fully combined and not clumpy.

Heat a large skillet or griddle over medium heat and coat with oil. Add about ⅓ cup pancake batter and cook until batter is bubbling, about 2 minutes. Flip and cook for an additional minute. Repeat for all pancakes and serve with citrus slices and powdered sugar.

Cinnamon Toast Crunch™ Cakes

DIFFICULTY: 1

Breakfast cereals have a reputation for being easy and quick. With just a small amount of extra effort, we wanted to transform a favorite cereal into something more substantial.

1 cup flour

2 tablespoons sugar

2 teaspoons baking powder

2 teaspoons cinnamon, divided

½ teaspoon salt

1 cup Cinnamon Toast Crunch™ cereal, crushed + ¼ cup for topping

1¼ cups buttermilk

3 tablespoons butter, melted

1 large egg

1 teaspoon vanilla extract

¼ cup maple syrup

In a small bowl, whisk together flour, sugar, baking powder, 1 teaspoon cinnamon, and salt. Stir crushed Cinnamon Toast Crunch™ cereal into mixture.

In a medium bowl, whisk together buttermilk, melted butter, egg, and vanilla. Add the dry ingredients into the wet ingredients, stirring until they're just combined, being careful not to over mix.

Heat a skillet or griddle over medium heat and pour about ¼ cup batter for each pancake. Cook pancakes for about 2 minutes on each side, until nicely browned. Repeat with all batter.

Stir the remaining 1 teaspoon cinnamon into the maple syrup and serve syrup over a stack of pancakes. Sprinkle remaining cereal over top.

Wholesome Sunflower Pancakes with Maple Bourbon Berries

DIFFICULTY: 2

We would like to stress that toasting nuts and seeds enriches and transforms their flavor. That being said, you can easily substitute sunflower seeds for walnuts or pecans in this recipe if they are more readily available. We doubled down on nuttiness by using whole wheat flour, but you can also lighten the flavor with all-purpose flour.

PANCAKES

1 cup whole wheat flour

½ cup sunflower seeds

1 teaspoon baking
   powder

¼ teaspoon salt

2 teaspoons maple syrup

2 eggs

1 tablespoon oil

½–¾ cup milk

TOPPING

2 cups strawberries,
   sliced

½ cup bourbon*

¼ cup maple syrup

* If prefered, you may leave the
  bourbon out altogether, cooking
  strawberries the same way with
  maple syrup.

In a small saucepan, add bourbon and cook over medium heat until reduced by half. Add in strawberries and maple syrup, reduce to medium-low heat, and let strawberries simmer until soft and liquid has reduced, about 10 minutes.

Lightly toast sunflower seeds in a skillet for 3–4 minutes over medium low heat. Remove and place in a food processor, pulsing until you have a well-chopped, but not fine, flour.

In a medium bowl, combine sunflower seed grinds, flour, baking powder, and salt. In a separate bowl, whisk together maple syrup, eggs, oil, and ½ cup milk. Pour over dry ingredients, stir just until combined-don't over mix. Add more milk if too thick to pour.

Heat a skillet over medium heat and spray or grease with oil. Pour ¼ cup batter and cook for 1–2 minutes until bubbles form. Flip and let cook for another 1–2 minutes until the pancake is cooked through.

Serve warm with cooked strawberries.

Guinness Pancakes

DIFFICULTY: 1

These pancakes are exactly what you would expect, and a little bit more, because we added chocolate chips. The flavor of the Guinness comes through perfectly. Feel free to serve with an almost full can of Guinness that might be laying around.

1½ cups flour

2 tablespoons sugar

1 tablespoon cocoa powder

1 teaspoon baking powder

½ teaspoon baking soda

½ teaspoon salt

1 egg

½ cup milk

½ cup Guinness

1 teaspoon vanilla extract

2 tablespoons butter, melted

⅓ cup dark chocolate chips

In a large mixing bowl, combine flour, sugar, cocoa powder, baking powder, baking soda and salt.

In a small bowl, whisk together milk and Guinness. Make a well in the center of the dry mixture and crack in your egg. Gradually add the liquids, whisking as you go.* Finally add in the vanilla extract. Fold in chocolate chips.

Heat a skillet over medium heat and grease well with spray or butter. Spoon batter to desired pancake size. When the first side forms air bubbles, flip the pancake and continue to cook through, about 1–2 minutes. Serve with whipped cream or maple syrup (or a glass of the leftover Guinness).

* *Gradually adding the ingredients and gently folding in the chips is essential to keep the carbonation.*

International Pancakes

As mentioned earlier, pancakes have been around for millennia—and don't look to be leaving anytime soon, either! Given the ample time there's been for word to spread, it's no surprise that unique versions of the pancake can be found in many cultures. So in this chapter, we'll be paying homage to the best international interpretations of pancakes from countries around the world!

Mini German Apple Pancakes

DIFFICULTY: 3

The base for these pancakes cooks very similarly to a Dutch Baby, or popover, needing a deeper pan to allow room for puffing up. We decided to make a bunch of mini German pancakes in muffin tins because 1) Mini food is always fun, and 2) You will have perfect serving sizes to handout to a multitude of people.

   This is listed as level 3 difficulty because there is a bit of preparation and 3 different processes to make it all come together. Rest assured, bakers of any skill level will be getting a little messy and enjoy making these.

GERMAN PANCAKE

1 cup milk

1 cup all-purpose flour

6 eggs at room
    temperature

½ teaspoon salt

1 teaspoon vanilla extract

¼ cup unsalted butter,
    melted

APPLE FILLING

4 Granny Smith apples,
    peeled, and chopped

2 tablespoons butter

½ teaspoon cinnamon

½ teaspoon lemon juice
    (or citric acid)

¼ cup light brown sugar,
    packed

CRUMB TOPPING

⅓ cup light brown sugar,
    packed

⅓ cup all-purpose flour

¼ cup oats

½ teaspoon ground
    cinnamon

3 tablespoons unsalted
    butter, chilled and cut
    into pieces

Preheat the oven to 400° and grease muffin tins with nonstick cooking spray with flour in it, or grease and flour pan, or use nonstick cooking spray *and* melted butter. These babies like to stick!

   In a large bowl, combine all German Pancake ingredients except the butter and whisk until smooth. Add butter and whisk until combined. Distribute batter evenly into tins (about ½ full). Bake for 20 minutes or until golden brown around the edges. They will be very puffy but will deflate as they cool.

While pancakes are baking and resting, melt 2 tablespoons butter in a large skillet over medium heat. Add apples, cinnamon, lemon juice and brown sugar and cook, stirring occasionally, until apples are tender and liquid is absorbed, approximately 8–10 minutes.

While the apples are cooking, combine the sugar, flour, oats, cinnamon, and butter, in a food processor and pulse into the mixture that is crumbly. You can also use a pastry cutter to incorporate the butter.

To assemble, evenly spoon cooked apples into German Pancake Bowls then top with Crumb Topping (this will be messy, embrace it). Broil for 3–6 minutes, rotating the pan halfway through so the topping browns evenly. Remove when crumbs are golden.

Japanese Souffle Pancakes
DIFFICULTY: 4

Souffle pancakes are unbelievably airy and unlike any other pancake in this book but making them is not for the faint of spatula. Pay careful attention to the low heat of your skillet to ensure the pancakes do not cook too quickly.

Pancakes Make People Happy

YOLK

1 egg yolk

1 tablespoon sugar

2 tablespoons milk

3 tablespoons flour

¼ teaspoon baking
   powder

WHITE

2 large egg whites

⅛ teaspoons cream
   of tartar

1½ tablespoons sugar

Whisk egg yolk with 1 tablespoon of sugar until pale and frothy. Mix the milk in batches. Sift the flour and baking powder over the yolk mixture and whisk well.

Whip the egg whites with the cream of tartar until frothy and pale, adding in the sugar gradually until the whites are whipped into a glossy thick meringue that holds a peak. Be careful not to over-whip.

Incorporate ⅓ whipped egg whites and whisk it into the bowl with the yolks until completely incorporated. Add half of the remaining whites and carefully whisk into the yolk batter, doing your best not to lose the volume of the egg whites. Add remaining egg whites and fold together.

Heat up a large nonstick frying pan over low heat. Lightly brush with oil and use a paper towel to rub it around. You'll want a very light film.

Using an ice cream scoop or measuring cup, scoop the batter onto the pan. An icing tube also works well for even, round batter. Scoop or pipe the batter onto the pan, cover and cook for 4–5 minutes. If you have a griddle with a lid that will cover the entire thing without touching the pancakes, use that on the lowest setting.

Remove the lid and add some more batter on top of each pancake. Cover and continue to cook for 4–5 more minutes. Lift the lid and use a spatula to gently peek under the pancake. The pancake should be released easily—don't force it.

If you still have any batter left, pile it on top of the pancakes and then gently flip. Cover and cook for 5–6 minutes. Pancakes will grow even taller and fluffier when done. Once the pancakes are golden and cooked through, gently remove and serve on a plate with powdered sugar and butter.

Scottish Oat Cakes

DIFFICULTY: 1

Your typical oatmeal breakfast would rarely include lemon, but combined in these chewy pancakes is a delightful combination. If oatmeal isn't a crowd pleaser in your house, making oatcakes might just change the game.

1 cup rolled oats

1 cup whole milk*

1 teaspoon lemon zest

3 teaspoons lemon juice

1 teaspoon honey, or to taste

1 large egg

¼ teaspoon fine salt

¼ teaspoon baking soda

¼ cup self-rising flour

Butter, for greasing

* Milk can be substituted for any milk preference, or water.

Bring oats and milk to a simmer in a pot over medium-high heat. Stir and cook for 1 minute and turn off the heat. Let cool down to room temperature, at least 10 minutes. Transfer oat mixture into a bowl. Add lemon zest and lemon juice. Add egg, honey, salt and baking soda.

Mix thoroughly with a spatula. Stir in flour until no dry spots remain. Cover and let rest for at least 1 hour.

Heat butter in a skillet over medium heat. Scoop spoonfuls of oat mixture into the hot skillet and flatten to desired thickness. Cook until browned and tops spring back when touched, 3 to 4 minutes per side.

Cachapa (Venezuelan Corn Pancakes)

DIFFICULTY: 3

Just pronouncing the name of this dish earns it its Difficulty level 3. Pronounced *kah-CHAH-pah*, the word means crumpet in Spanish, and they are traditional road-side stand food in Venezuela. The most traditional ingredients would be maize and queso de mano, but standard cornmeal and any soft white cheese will suffice. They will come together like cornmeal grilled cheese. A bit of intuition is needed when judging the pasty-ness of your batter. Corn can hold different amounts of water; you just want to ensure a sticky consistency that won't spread too much.

4 cups frozen or canned corn kernels, drained

½ cup flour

½ cup heavy cream

¼ cup milk

1 tablespoon sugar

1 teaspoon salt

¼ teaspoon cayenne pepper

½ cup cornmeal

2 tablespoons chopped red pepper (or jalapeno if you like spicy)

1½ cups grated mozzarella or good white melting cheese (queso de mano would be most authentic)

Butter, for greasing

Set aside ¼ cup of corn. Put the remaining ingredients, except for butter and cheese, in a blender and blend until a thick paste forms.

Add the rest of the corn kernels and stir. Let stand for about 5 minutes for the mixture to thicken.

Preheat a pan or griddle over medium heat and grease. Make each cachapa using ⅓ cup of the mixture at a time, making a circle of about 4 inches. Cook for 4–5 minutes and turn.

Cook for 3 more minutes until the cachapas are golden brown. Remove from heat for 1 minute, then place one pancake back on the griddle, heap with ½ cup cheese, and cover with another pancake. After 2 minutes, press the 'sandwich' down with the back of a spatula to make sure melting cheese is evenly distributed. When cheese is fully melted, remove from heat and enjoy.

Shou Zhua Bing Chinese Pancakes

DIFFICULTY: 4

If this is your first time making Shou Zhua Bing, know that it is a recipe that requires a bit of technique. Not to worry; with practice, you'll soon be a master so don't be too hard on yourself if the first ones aren't just right. Focus on one component at a time. The chewy, spicy layers of these pancakes are worth a try.

3 tablespoons oil

4 scallions, chopped in half

½ teaspoon anise seed or three star anise*

½ teaspoon pepper or whole peppercorns*

3 tablespoons flour

⅛ teaspoon ginger*

⅛ teaspoon ground clove or 1 tablespoon whole clove*

FOR THE DOUGH

2½ cups flour

½ teaspoon salt

¼ cup boiling water

¾ cup cold water

TO ASSEMBLE

2 tablespoons sesame seeds

¼ cup finely chopped scallions

Salt (to taste)

Make the flavored roux

In a small saucepan over low heat, add the oil. Throw in the scallion pieces and all spices. Keep the pan over low heat for about 10 minutes, until fragrant. Pick out all the whole spices and scallions so you are left with infused oil. Stir in the flour to create a thin roux. Set it aside, and let it cool completely.

Make the dough

In a mixing bowl, combine the flour and salt. Make a well in the flour and add the boiling water, mix until incorporated. Gradually add the cold water and knead everything together to form a smooth dough ball. Try not to over-knead. Cover with a damp cloth and let it rest for 30 minutes.

To assemble

Divide the dough into 4–6 equal pieces. Roll each piece of dough into a long rope with hands, and then use a rolling pin to roll it flat. Brush a thin layer of the roux all over the dough, and then sprinkle it sparingly with sesame seeds, chopped scallion, and salt.

* The spices in this recipe can be substituted for with 5-spice powder.

Start on one end and roll the dough up. Stand the roll upright and press it down with your palm. Lightly roll out the resulting circle until you get a pancake that's between ¼–½-inch thick. It's ok of the outer edges break open a bit. Repeat for each pancake.

To cook the pancakes

Heat a pan over medium heat and add a tablespoon or two of oil. Place the pancake in the pan. Once the bottom starts to turn a little golden, add two teaspoons of water to the sides of the pan (don't pour the water on the pancake), and immediately cover with a lid. Cook for 3 minutes. Uncover the pan, flip the pancake, and do the same steps with the other side.

To finish, uncover the lid again, turn up the heat slightly, and brown both sides while flipping the pancake occasionally. When it's golden brown, use forks to squeeze and pinch the pancake a couple times to loosen the layers and create a flakier pancake, because you ideally want to see the layers when you hand-pull it apart. The cooked pancakes should be crispy and slightly chewy.

Korean Shrimp Pancakes

DIFFICULTY: 3

As far as pancakes go, these are high on the fiber and protein list. Packed with vegetables and shrimp, these make a great all in one dinner dish.

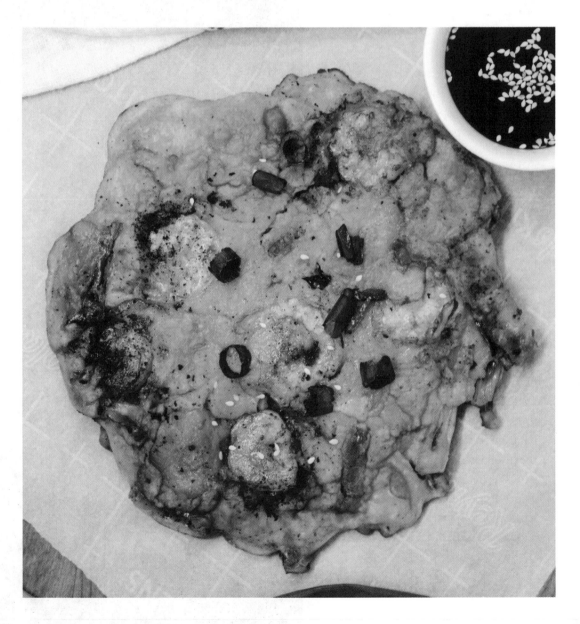

Pancakes Make People Happy

PANCAKES

1 cup flour

2 tablespoons cornstarch

½ teaspoon onion powder

½ teaspoon garlic powder

½ teaspoon sugar

⅔ teaspoon salt

¼ teaspoon pepper

1 cup milk
(can substitute water)

1 egg

12 medium raw, peeled
and deveined shrimp
(can also use precooked)

10 thin green onions, cut
into 2-inch lengths,
white parts halved
lengthwise

2 medium carrots, super
thinly sliced

Butter or oil for frying

SAUCE

2 tablespoons soy sauce

2 teaspoons rice vinegar

½ teaspoon sugar

½ teaspoon sesame seeds

Dash of chili flakes

Add a generous coat of oil to the bottom of a 10-inch cast iron pan. Turn the heat to medium to preheat the pan. In a bowl, whisk together the flour, cornstarch, onion powder, garlic powder, sugar and salt.

Add the milk or water to the dry mix, crack the egg and combine until smooth. Do not over mix or gluten may form and your pancake will be tough.

Sprinkle some salt and flour onto the carrots and green onions. Add the carrots and green onions to the batter and stir. There should be some vegetables that can't 'fit' in the batter, basically a very clumpy toss of vegetables coated in batter.

When oil is almost smoking, pour half the batter in. It should be sizzling. Work quickly to spread the batter and vegetables to make sure they're even and not too thick. Too thick of a pancake is difficult to cook through. Top the pancake with ½ shrimp. Push down the shrimp so that it is snug in the batter.

Fry for 3–4 minutes or until the bottom is crisp and brown. Shrimp will start to turn a little pink (if using raw) and the pancake will have almost set.

Carefully flip the pancake, swirl some oil, shake the pan so the oil reaches the bottom of the pancake. Using the spatula, gently but firmly press down the pancake to make sure the bottom of the pancake is in contact with the hot pan. Fry for another 4–5 minutes. Carefully check to see if the shrimp and batter is cooked through. Fry until it is cooked through.

Malaysian Peanut Pancake Turnover (Apam Balik)

DIFFICULTY: 3

Foods that need to rise are usually well worth it, right? Pizza, English muffins, cinnamon rolls… These Eastern turnovers are packed with peanuts and sugar, and voluminous enough to share.

PANCAKES

2 cups flour

5 tablespoons sugar

1 packet active dry yeast

¼ teaspoon baking powder

⅛ teaspoon baking soda

½ teaspoon salt

1½ cup warm milk

2 eggs, room temperature

Butter for cooking

FILLING

1½ cups ground roasted peanuts (coarse or fine is up to you)

4 tablespoons brown sugar

4 tablespoons sugar

Butter

In a bowl, add all the ingredients for the batter and whisk until smooth. Cover the bowl and let rise for 2–3 hours (or overnight in the refrigerator). Batter will increase in volume and the surface will start to bubble. If you had chilled the batter overnight, let it sit at room temperature for 30 minutes.

Heat a skillet over medium heat and coat with butter or oil. Give batter a stir, then pour the batter depending on how thick you want the pancake to be and spread it evenly. If you like your pancake edges a little crusty, swivel the pan so that some batter coats the side of the pan.

Let the pancake cook until you see bubbles appearing on the surface and the pancake has started to set. To speed up this process, cover the pan with a lid.

Once the surface has started to set, add small dollops of butter all around the surface. Sprinkle with a portion of the filling respective to the amount of batter you poured. When the bottom has a golden-brown color to it and the pancake has completely set, fold the pancake in half like a moon shape and remove from the pan (have no fear, it's like closing a big omelet. If some peanuts fall out, just toss them on the plate.) If you leave it much longer, the pancake will dry out. Repeat with the remaining batter. Slice and serve immediately, especially delicious with whipped cream or vanilla ice cream.

Austrian Torn Fluffy Pancake
(Kaiserschmarrn)

DIFFICULTY: 3

Kaiserschmarrn were made popular by an Austrian Emperor who loved sweet pancakes for dessert. Can't say we blame him. The success of this pancake relies on paying attention to the doneness, resulting in both a custardy and crunchy pancake reminiscent of fried dough from a county fair.

PANCAKES

½ cup raisins

2 tablespoons dark fruit juice*

4 large eggs, separated

2 tablespoons sugar

¼ teaspoon salt

1 teaspoon baking powder

¾ cup flour

½ cup milk, any kind

2-3 tablespoons butter for skillet (don't skimp)

Powdered sugar for topping

* We used elderberry juice for our raisins, but you can omit raisins all together if you prefer.

First, soak raisins in chosen juice while batter is made.

In a large bowl, whisk together egg yolks, sugar, salt, and baking powder. Whisk in milk, then flour, whisking until incorporated, a few lumps are fine. Let rest for 10 minutes. Meanwhile, in a second medium bowl with an electric mixer, beat egg whites until they form stiff peaks. Fold into egg yolk mixture, trying not to deflate the egg whites. Thoroughly dry raisins, and gently fold in.

Heat a skillet over medium heat. Add 2–3 tablespoons of butter and let melt. Skillet should be thickly coated. Pour batter into pan and spread smooth. Cook for 3–4 minutes, lifting an edge to peek occasionally, until it's a deep golden-brown underneath; reduce the heat if it's browning very quickly. To successfully flip the pancake, make sure all the sides are loosened from the skillet. With a large enough spatula, flip the pancake. Alternatively, you can slide the pancake onto a plate, invert your skillet with a potholder over the plate, and toss the pancake back into the skillet. Continue cooking until deeply golden underneath on the second side, about 3 minutes.

Your pancake should NOT be fully cooked through when you remove it from the skillet. To tear/chop up the pancake, use the edge of a sharp spatula or a fork and knife to cut into 1–2-inch pieces. The goal is to get pieces that are crispy on the outside, but soft and runny on the inside. To crisp a bit more, you can toss pieces back in the skillet with a bit more butter, but a custardy center in each bite is ideal. Sprinkle with powdered sugar and serve immediately.

Indian Chai Spice Pancakes
with Black Tea Poached Pear

DIFFICULTY: 3

Chai spice is warming and aromatic, making these pancakes extra comforting (they'll also make your kitchen smell amazing).

SPICED MILK

1 cup milk

2 teaspoons ground ginger

4 cinnamon sticks

2 teaspoons freshly ground nutmeg

2 star anise

2 teaspoons cloves

2 teaspoons ground cardamom

1 teaspoon black peppercorns

PANCAKES

8 ounces spice-infused milk

2 eggs

½ stick butter, melted

1 teaspoon vanilla

1 cup flour

2 tablespoons sugar

2 teaspoons baking powder

1 teaspoon salt

POACHED PEARS

1 red pear

1 black tea bag

3 cups water

1 teaspoon vanilla extract

¼ cup sugar

In a small saucepan, combine the milk, ground ginger, cinnamon sticks, ground nutmeg, and star anise.* Bring the milk to a simmer, cover with lid, remove from heat, and let steep and cool, about 10 minutes. Strain.

Slice the pear into ½-inch thick slices. Peel if desired. In a pot with a lid, combine the black tea bag, vanilla, and water and bring to a boil with the lid on.

Poach the pear in the tea for 3–5 minutes until fork-tender, then remove from the poaching liquid.

Combine spice-infused milk, eggs, melted butter, and vanilla extract in a bowl and whisk thoroughly. Add the flour, sugar, baking powder,

* If you do not have the spices for chai spice, you can steep chai tea in hot milk.

and salt and mix until smooth. Batter should be thick and fluffy. Heat a skillet or griddle over medium heat and lightly grease. Pour batter to desired pancake size, cooking until bubbles form (about 2 minutes), then flip. Cook until golden brown on both sides. Serve with poached pears.

Farinata

DIFFICULTY: 1

Chickpea flour is just ground chickpeas and can also be called gram or besan flour when you are searching the shelves. Just like chickpeas, it is a good source of protein, potassium and fiber. Another bonus for some is that farinata is gluten free, dairy free, and incredibly easy.

Pancakes Make People Happy

1 cup chickpea flour*

1⅓ cups water

1 teaspoon salt

2 tablespoons olive oil

½ small onion, thinly sliced

1 tablespoon dried rosemary

Pepper

* You can make your own chickpea flour with the bags of dried chickpeas in the store if you cannot find chickpea flour. Just run them through a food processor until fine.

Whisk the chickpea flour and water together in a medium bowl. Whisk in the salt and olive oil. Cover mixture and let sit at room temperature for at least 1 hour and up to 12 hours or overnight.

Sautee the thinly sliced onion in olive oil until soft but not browned. Add rosemary just before onions are done cooking and stir. Add cooked onions to chickpea flour mixture.

Heat oven to 400°F. In a 10.5-inch cast iron skillet or oven-proof skillet, heat a few tablespoons of olive oil over medium high heat. When the oil is hot, add the batter to the skillet. Transfer to the oven and cook for about 40 minutes or until a knife inserted into the center comes out clean. Place the pancake under the broiler if the top is not browned for 1–2 minutes.

Remove the skillet from the oven and allow it to cool for a minute. You can carefully transfer the pancake to a cutting board, or can serve straight from the pan. Top with more olive oil and freshly ground pepper. Serve warm, cut into wedges.

Seasonal Pancakes

In this chapter, you will find recipes being referred to as "seasonal" for two different reasons: either the ingredients are available only at a certain time of year, or the recipe may be holiday-related and therefore most appropriate at a certain time of year. Either way, these pancakes make for a special treat to be savored during special times!

Pumpkin Pancakes with Maple Roasted Walnuts

DIFFICULTY: 1

If society has made any ingredient seasonal, it's pumpkin. As soon as fall comes around, it seems everything with flavor is available in pumpkin and we didn't want pancakes to be the exception. All squash (including pumpkin), pairs deliciously with maple and nuts, but be sure to keep a close eye on your toasting walnuts because they are quick to burn.

½ cup flour

½ teaspoon pumpkin pie spice

1 tablespoon sugar

¼ teaspoon salt

1 teaspoon baking powder

2 eggs

2 tablespoons butter, melted

½ teaspoon vanilla extract

½ cup milk

½ cup pumpkin puree

⅓ cup walnuts (optional)

Maple syrup

Oil or spray for greasing

Whisk the chickpea flour and water together in a medium bowl. Whisk in the salt and olive oil. Cover mixture and let sit at room temperature for at least 1 hour and up to 12 hours or overnight.

If topping with walnuts, toss raw nuts with maple syrup until well coated. Toast on medium heat in a pan, or on a sheet pan in the oven at 400° while pancakes cook. Check frequently until syrup is crystallizing around the nuts.

In a large bowl mix together flour, pumpkin pie spice, sugar, salt and baking powder.

In a smaller bowl mix eggs, butter, vanilla, milk and pumpkin.

Add wet ingredients to the dry and mix until smooth. If you think the batter is too runny at this point, add a little bit more flour (1–2 tablespoons) until thicker. Heat a pan or griddle to medium heat, spray or coat with oil. Pour ⅓ cup batter and cook pancakes until golden brown and bubbles start to form, then flip and cook until brown on the second side. Top with walnuts and additional maple syrup.

Apple Cider Pancakes
with Caramel Apple Syrup

DIFFICULTY: 2

Every fall we become cider enthusiasts because we love making apple cider with our old-fashioned press. The caramel apple syrup used to top these pancakes is especially delicious, tasting like the best part of a caramel apple on top of sweet apple pancakes.

PANCAKES

2 cups all-purpose flour

2 tablespoons sugar

2 teaspoons baking powder

1 teaspoon baking soda

¼ teaspoon salt

1 cup Greek vanilla yogurt

1 cup apple cider

2 eggs, separated

CARAMEL APPLE SYRUP

¼ cup butter

¼ cup apple cider

1 cup brown sugar

In a large bowl, combine flour, sugar, baking powder, baking soda and salt.

In another bowl, combine yogurt, cider and egg yolks. Add dry ingredients to wet ingredients and mix until just combined.

In a third bowl, beat egg whites until stiff peaks form. Add ¼ of the egg whites into the batter and stir in. Add remaining egg whites and fold in, until just combined.

Heat a griddle over medium heat. Spray with nonstick cooking spray or melt a small amount of butter on the griddle. Pour batter by ¼-cupfuls onto the hot griddle. Turn pancakes when bubbles form on top, then cook a minute or two longer, until the second side is golden brown.

In a small saucepan, melt the butter. Add in the apple cider, then stir in brown sugar. Cook, whisking, until it comes to a boil. Boil for 1 minute, whisking constantly. Serve warm.

Eggnog Pancakes

DIFFICULTY: 2

Eggnog has always been a winter holiday drink because it is enjoyed hot, giving off warm aromas of nutmeg, vanilla and cinnamon. It's incredibly indulgent, but we've decided to include eggnog in both the batter and the glaze of these pancakes to ensure an unmistakable plate of eggnog flavor.

PANCAKES

2 cups flour

1 tablespoon baking
   powder

½ teaspoon salt

¼ teaspoon nutmeg

2 eggs

1 teaspoon vanilla

2 tablespoons butter
   melted

2-2½ cups eggnog

GLAZE

1 cup powdered sugar

2-3 tablespoons eggnog

¼ teaspoon nutmeg

In a large bowl, whisk together flour, baking powder, salt and nutmeg.

In a medium bowl, whisk together eggs, vanilla and melted butter. Whisk in 2 cups eggnog. Add wet ingredients to dry ingredients and stir until smooth. If needed, add additional eggnog, a little bit at a time, until batter reaches desired consistency.

Heat a griddle over medium heat. Spray with nonstick cooking spray or melt a small amount of butter on the griddle. Pour batter by ¼-cupfuls. Turn pancakes when bubbles form on top, then cook a minute or two longer, until the second side is golden brown.

Serve pancakes warm, drizzled with glaze.

Lofty Gingerbread Pancakes

DIFFICULTY: 2

If you only make a few recipes in this book, make this one of them. It's gingerbread to perfection. Nothing will bring back childhood holiday memories quicker than Lofty Gingerbread Pancakes.

PANCAKES

1 cup all-purpose flour

2 tablespoons brown sugar

2 tablespoons granulated sugar

2 teaspoons cinnamon

1 teaspoon ground ginger

1 teaspoon allspice

1 teaspoon ground nutmeg

1 teaspoon baking powder

1 teaspoon baking soda

½ teaspoon ground cloves

Pinch of salt

¾ cup buttermilk (or ¾ cup milk + a shy tablespoon of vinegar)

1 large egg

3 tablespoons molasses

1 tablespoon canola or vegetable oil

1 teaspoon vanilla extract

GLAZE

1 cup powdered sugar

2 tablespoons butter

½ teaspoon vanilla

1-2 tablespoons milk

In a medium bowl, beat together all glaze ingredients and set aside. In a large mixing bowl, add the first 11 ingredients, through optional salt, and whisk to combine; set aside.

In a medium bowl, add the remaining five ingredients, through vanilla, and whisk to combine.

Pour wet mixture over dry ingredients, stirring until just combined. Batter will be fairly thick and lumpy; do not try to stir out lumps.

Pre-heat a skillet over medium heat and spray with cooking spray (or use melted butter).

Scoop batter onto skillet or griddle for pancakes of desired size. Cook for about 2½–3 minutes. Flip when underside is golden, cooking for an additional 2 minutes. Repeat the process with the remaining batter, adding more cooking spray to the skillet as needed. Serve with generous glaze and enjoy.

Butternut Griddle Biscuits
with Sage Brown Butter

DIFFICULTY: 2

This recipe happened quite by accident, but once we'd made it we couldn't stop sampling them! These are considered seasonal because butternut squash ripens in the fall and you must use fresh sage before the winter frost.

PANCAKES

1 cup roasted and mashed butternut squash

⅓ cup yogurt or sour cream

2 large eggs

½ cup grated hard cheese (we used parmesan)

¾ teaspoon salt

A few grinds of black pepper

1 teaspoon baking powder

1 cup flour

Butter or olive oil for griddle

SAGE BROWN BUTTER

3 tablespoons butter

A pinch or two of salt

Fresh sage leaves

In a large bowl, whisk squash, yogurt, eggs, cheese, salt, pepper and baking powder until smooth. Add flour and stir until just combined. Batter will be thick.

Heat a large pan or griddle over medium heat. Grease with butter or olive oil. Spoon on pancake batter, a heaped soup spoon or scant ¼ cup at a time (our cakes were about 2½ inches wide). Press the back of the batter mound to flatten the pancake slightly. Cook until golden brown underneath, flip, and cook until golden brown on the second side. Pancakes should have no give left when you press on them to indicate they are cooked through.

For butter, add butter ingredients to a small pan on medium heat. Cook until butter is bubbling and thoroughly browned (not burnt) and sage leaves have crisped a bit. Pour leaves and butter over pancakes (yes, drenched in butter) and enjoy.

Pink Heart Beet Pancakes

DIFFICULTY: 2

This can be a very romantic recipe for Valentine's day, especially if you make them heart shaped. We used a heart mold with handle attachment for lifting off the griddle once the pancake is poured. It's a bit tricky but be sure and non-stick spray the mold before each use.

1 medium to large beet,
   boiled and peeled

1 cup milk

1 large egg

1 tablespoon melted
   butter

½ teaspoon vanilla
   extract

2 tablespoons maple
   syrup

1 cup flour

1 tablespoon baking
   powder

¼ teaspoon salt

Oil for greasing

Heavy cream for topping
   (optional)

Strawberries for topping
   (optional)

In a blender, puree beet with milk until smooth. Add egg, butter, vanilla extract and maple syrup, and blend to combine. Add flour, baking powder and salt to the mixture. Pulse to combine (try not to over blend).

Heat a griddle over medium heat and grease with oil or butter. Pour ⅓ cup of the batter into your heart mold, or onto the griddle. Cook for 2–3 minutes, until small bubbles start to form on the top and the edges firm up.

Remove heart mold carefully before flipping or flip the regular pancakes and cook for another 1–2 minutes until the pancakes are cooked through. If using the mold, don't worry if it doesn't come off perfect, you can use a spatula or knife to trim the edges a bit.

Repeat for the remaining batter. If serving with whipped cream, beat heavy cream until thick and dollop on pancakes with a few berries.

Peachy Summer Dutch Baby

DIFFICULTY: 3

These will make you say, "Ooh, La-La!" Definitely worth the extra effort.

4 eggs

1 cup whole milk

1 cup flour

1 teaspoon vanilla

4 tablespoons sugar

½ teaspoon salt

1 teaspoon cinnamon

½ teaspoon nutmeg

1 teaspoon lime zest

¼ cup chopped pecans

3 ripe peaches or 8 ounces frozen peach slices, thawed

4 tablespoons butter

Powdered sugar (for serving)

Pecans (for serving)

Preheat the oven to 425°F. In a stand mixer, add eggs, milk, flour, vanilla, sugar, salt, cinnamon and nutmeg and mix until smooth. Stir in the lime zest and pecans.

If using fresh peaches, bring a pot of water to a boil. Cut an "X" into the base of the peach and boil for 1 minute. Remove with a slotted spoon and transfer to a bowl of ice water.

Once cool enough to handle, gently rub off skins. Cut into ¼-inch thick slices, discarding the pits.

In a large cast iron skillet, melt butter on low heat. Add the peaches. Pour batter over the peaches and bake in the oven for 20–25 minutes or until the pancake is lightly browned and puffy.

Dust with powdered sugar and chopped pecans and serve immediately.

Christmas Tree Stack

DIFFICULTY: 1

This is the best recipe to make with children. They'll enjoy the challenge of making the different sized circles required for the stack.

1½ cups flour

1 teaspoon baking powder

1 tablespoon chia seeds

Pinch of salt

1 tablespoon chlorella powder, spirulina powder, matcha, or green food coloring.

1 cup milk

2 tablespoons maple syrup

1 teaspoon vanilla extract

1 banana, mashed

1 tablespoon oil or spray

1 strawberry (or raspberry or pomegranate seeds, for color, optional)

Powdered sugar for topping (optional)

Mix dry ingredients. Add wet ingredients and mix until combined. Depending on which ingredient you are using for green color, add as much until desired shade.

Heat a griddle or skillet on medium heat and coat with oil. Spoon batter onto pan, starting with a large circle for the tree base. Each pancake will get smaller and smaller to make the tree.

Heat pancakes until bubbles form, then flip. Cook until lightly browned on both sides.

Stack pancakes in the shape of a tree. Add tree topper strawberry and a sprinkle of powdered sugar, served with maple syrup.

Cornmeal Cakes with Green Tomato Chutney

DIFFICULTY: 3

In midsummer, everybody's hankering for vegetables fresh-off-the-vine, and green tomatoes fit the bill. The chutney that is served with these cornmeal cakes is best described as straight out of a summer picnic. If you can, make it a day ahead so the flavors have a chance to blend.

GREEN TOMATO CHUTNEY

2 cups chopped green tomatoes

½ cup chopped red onion

⅓ cup packed brown sugar

¼ cup raisins

¼ cup cider vinegar

1 tablespoon mustard seed

1 teaspoon ground ginger

½ teaspoon chili pepper flakes

½ teaspoon fennel seed

½ teaspoon salt

¼ teaspoon ground allspice

⅛ teaspoon cinnamon

PANCAKES

2 cups yellow cornmeal

1 teaspoon sugar

½ teaspoon salt

1½–2 cups boiling water

Vegetable oil for frying

To make the cakes, combine cornmeal, sugar, and salt in a medium bowl. Pour 1½ cups of boiling water over the mixture and stir. Batter should be on the thicker side, but if needed, add up to 2 cups of water. Heat oil in a cast iron skillet over medium-high heat. Drop about 2 tablespoons of batter for each cake in the pan. Cook until golden brown, about 2–3 minutes each side. Place on a paper towel-lined plate to soak up oil until ready to serve.

To make the chutney, combine all ingredients in a medium saucepan over medium-high heat. Bring mixture to a boil, stir, and reduce to a simmer. Cover and cook until tomatoes and onions have softened, about 15–20 minutes. Remove from heat and bring to room temperature. Serve over hot cornmeal cakes.

Red, White, & Blue Pancakes

DIFFICULTY: 2

Pie is traditionally the centerpiece of a Fourth of July picnic, but even at a Difficulty of 2, we think these are easy as pie! The blue cornmeal will be a necessity, if your regular supermarket doesn't have it, you may have to look at a local food co-op or source it on the internet. Please take the time to make the real whipped cream—it really isn't the same without it.

WHIPPED CREAM

1 cup heavy cream

¼ cup sour cream

½ teaspoon vanilla

PANCAKES

1½ cups fine-ground
   blue cornmeal

1½ cups boiling water

1½ cups flour

2 teaspoons baking
   powder

1½ teaspoons salt

¾ teaspoon baking soda

4 eggs, beaten

¾ cup whole milk

½ cup butter, melted

Fresh raspberries or
   strawberries

To make the whipped cream, beat heavy cream, sour cream, and vanilla with a stand or hand mixer until medium peaks form, about 2–3 minutes. Chill until ready to serve.

To make pancakes, stir together blue cornmeal and boiling water in a medium bowl until no dry cornmeal remains. Cover mixture with plastic wrap and let stand for 15 minutes.

In a large bowl, combine flour, baking powder, salt, and baking soda. Add eggs, milk, and melted butter and whisk to combine. Whisk in blue cornmeal mixture until just combined.

Heat griddle to medium heat and grease with butter. Scoop ¼ cup of batter onto heated griddle. Cook until bubbles form and sides of pancakes look set, about 2–3 minutes. Flip and cook another 2–3 minutes. Continue with remaining batter. Top pancakes with prepared whipped cream and fresh red berries, if desired.

Berry Ombre Pancakes

DIFFICULTY: 3

If you are feeling creative and really want to impress your friends, then today is the perfect day for some Berry Ombre Pancakes. You'll have to pay close attention to measurements and directions to achieve the gradual colorful shading that makes these so outstanding.

2 cups flour

4 teaspoons baking powder

Salt

4 teaspoons maple syrup

4 teaspoons vegetable oil

2 cups whole milk (approximate)

1 teaspoon white vinegar

¾ cup raspberries, mashed

1 tablespoon blackberries, mashed

Whipped cream and fresh berries for serving

To make pancakes, take four medium bowls and set aside. In each bowl, place ½ cup flour, 1 teaspoon baking powder, a pinch of salt, 1 teaspoon maple syrup, and 1 teaspoon vegetable oil.

Leave the first bowl plain. In the second bowl, add a heaping tablespoon of mashed raspberries. In the third bowl add remaining mashed raspberries, reserving a tablespoon. In the fourth bowl, add remaining mashed raspberries and the tablespoon of mashed blackberries. Do not mix any of the batters yet.

For the first bowl (the plain batter), combine ¼ teaspoon vinegar with ½ cup milk and let stand for 1 minute. Add milk mixture to flour mixture and stir until just combined. Set aside.

For the second bowl, combine ¼ teaspoon vinegar with ⅓ cup milk and let stand for 1 minute. Add milk mixture to flour mixture and stir until just combined. Set aside.

For the third bowl, combine ¼ teaspoon vinegar to ¼ cup milk and let stand for 1 minute. Add milk mixture to flour mixture and stir until just combined.

For the fourth bowl, combine ¼ teaspoon vinegar with ¼ cup milk and let stand for 1 minute. Add milk mixture to flour mixture and stir until just combined. More milk may be needed for the second, third, and fourth batter mixture, but batter should be thick.

Heat a griddle over medium heat and coat with butter or nonstick spray. Starting with the fourth batter, scoop ¼ cup batter onto the hot griddle. Cook until the bottom is lightly browned and bubbles begin to form on the top. Flip, and cook until the second side is browned.

Continue with the third, second and first batters, for an ombre effect when pancakes are stacked. Each batter makes two pancakes. Top with whipped cream and fresh berries, if desired.

Apple Crisp Topped Pancakes

DIFFICULTY: 3

I'm not sure these are worth the trouble of making them…until you see the look on someone's face when they bite into one for the first time, that is.

FRUIT CRISP FILLING

1 large apple, diced

¼ cup dried cranberries

½ cup brown sugar

2 tablespoons flour

FRUIT CRISP TOPPING

1½ cup oats

4 tablespoons butter, softened

2 tablespoons flour

½ cup brown sugar

PANCAKES

One recipe Old Fashioned Buttermilk pancake batter (page 4)

Preheat the oven to 375°F. In a medium bowl, combine fruit crisp filling ingredients, and toss to combine. Spread fruit mixture in an 8x8-inch baking dish. In another medium bowl combine all fruit crisp topping ingredients and stir with a fork until mixture is crumbly. Top fruit with crumble topping. Bake fruit crisp until topping is browned and mixture is bubbling, 40–45 minutes.

Prepare pancake batter and cook pancakes on a greased griddle heated to medium heat. Top pancakes with prepared fruit crisp and ice cream or whipped cream, if desired. Extra fruit crisp can be covered and stored at room temperature for up to three days.

Dessert Pancakes

A chapter like this needs no explanation—"cake" is right there in the name! We would just like to express that pancakes can be celebratory, fun, and decadent desserts. We bet you'll recognize a few of these popularized dessert ideas.

Funfetti Pancakes

DIFFICULTY: 1

These are the perfect birthday pancakes, not only because they look like a birthday celebration, but because they taste like one too! We made the pancakes fairly large to resemble an actual birthday cake, but they would look great as a small stack as well. The topping for these pancakes couldn't get any easier either…just pop some vanilla frosting in the microwave and pour over the stack, and of course you can't forget the sprinkles!

1⅓ cups all-purpose flour

2 teaspoons baking powder

2 tablespoons granulated sugar

½ teaspoon salt

1 box Funfetti cake mix (found in most grocery stores)

⅓ cup canola oil

3 large eggs

2⅓ cups milk

1 container Funfetti icing (with the sprinkles on top)

In a large bowl, combine the flour, baking powder, sugar, salt and cake mix. Set aside.

In another small bowl, mix together the oil, eggs and milk. Add the wet ingredients into the dry ingredients and mix just until combined. The batter will be thick.

Heat a griddle to about 250–275°F (low heat so the pancakes do not burn). Spray the griddle with cooking spray. Ladle the pancake batter onto the hot pan and cook the pancakes for about 1–2 minutes or until bubbles start forming in the batter. We made plate-size pancakes to stack like a cake. They should be light and puffy. Flip the pancake and cook for an additional minute or until cooked through.

Microwave or heat about ½ cup of icing to pour on top of the pancake 'cake' stack. Sprinkle with sprinkles.

Lemon Poppyseed Pancakes

DIFFICULTY: 1

Lemon poppyseed is a well-known flavor combination often found in baked goods like muffins, but one which has since broadened its horizon to loaf breads, layer cakes and more. So we figured, why not pancakes?! Our version is bursting with both fresh lemon flavor and the soft crunch of poppyseeds and resembles the same texture as the classic muffin.

1 cup flour

2 teaspoons baking powder

½ teaspoon baking soda

½ cup whole milk

4 tablespoons yogurt

1 teaspoon vanilla extract

1 tablespoon sugar

2 tablespoons vegetable oil

Zest and juice of 1 medium lemon

Vanilla yogurt for topping

Mix the first three ingredients together in a large bowl. Stir in the remaining ingredients until well combined and the texture is runny but still thick.

Heat a griddle or nonstick pan to medium heat. Scoop about ¼ cup batter onto the griddle and cook for 1–2 minutes (until lightly browned) before carefully flipping onto the other side. Cook for another 1–2 minutes. Repeat with the rest of the batter.

Top with some vanilla yogurt and an extra dash of poppyseeds and lemon zest.

Cinnamon Roll Pancakes

DIFFICULTY: 2

The combination of the gooey cinnamon bun filling and glaze make these pancakes a great dessert choice. We chose to pour the cinnamon filling with a spoon, but using a piping bag or squirt bottle will make the swirl a little less organic in shape. The filling will leak a bit when you flip the pancake.

PANCAKES

1 cup flour

2 teaspoons baking powder

½ teaspoon sea salt

1 cup milk

2 tablespoons maple syrup

3 tablespoons butter, melted

5 tablespoons brown sugar

2 teaspoons ground cinnamon

Oil, for greasing

GLAZE

½ cup powdered sugar

1 tablespoon milk

In a large bowl, whisk together the flour, baking powder, and salt. In a small bowl, whisk together the milk and maple syrup. Add the wet ingredients to the dry and whisk to combine. Do not overmix.

In a small bowl, mix together the butter, brown sugar, and cinnamon. Transfer to a pastry bag or a cup with a pour spout.

Lightly grease a skillet or griddle and heat over medium heat. Pour half the batter for each pancake. Pipe or pour a circular swirl of the cinnamon mixture into the batter. When small bubbles appear in the center of the pancakes, after about 3 minutes, flip.

Cook on the other side for about 1 minute more, until lightly browned and cooked through. Once removed from heat, pour any remaining cinnamon mixture into the swirl crevices on the pancake. In a small bowl, combine the confectioners' sugar and water and whisk until smooth.

Drizzle the pancakes with the glaze and serve.

Pancakes Make People Happy

Sticky Toffee Pancakes

DIFFICULTY: 3

Sticky toffee pudding is a traditional English dessert, technically a cake, served hot and studded with dates. While our pancakes do not have any dates in them, a half cup of them, chopped, can easily be added to the rich molasses and spice batter. These pancakes should be served and eaten immediately because the toffee sauce hardens quickly.

TOFFEE SAUCE

½ cup brown sugar
½ cup honey
¼ cup heavy cream
3 tablespoons butter
1 teaspoon brandy
¼ teaspoon salt
¼ teaspoon vanilla extract

PANCAKES

1 large egg white + ⅛ teaspoon cream of tartar
1 cup whole milk
2 tablespoons molasses
1 large egg yolk
½ teaspoon ground ginger
2 tablespoons butter, melted
1¼ cups flour
1 tablespoon brown sugar
2½ teaspoons baking powder
¼ teaspoon ground cinnamon
¼ teaspoon ground allspice
Oil and butter for cooking

To make the sauce, combine brown sugar, honey, heavy cream, butter, brandy and salt in a small pot and set over medium heat. Bring to a gentle boil and cook for 3–4 minutes, stirring occasionally. Turn off the heat and stir in the vanilla extract, set aside.

To make the pancakes, in a medium bowl with handheld-mixer, whisk together egg white and cream of tartar on high speed until stiff peak forms. Set aside.

In another large bowl, whisk together whole milk, molasses, egg yolk and ginger until even. Add flour, brown sugar, baking powder, ground cinnamon and allspice right into the wet ingredients. Next, add the melted butter and stir everything together with a fork just until it comes into a thick batter. Fold the beaten egg white into the batter with a spatula in 3 additions, just until incorporated. Try not to overwork the batter too much.

Heat a skillet or griddle over medium heat, coat with butter or oil. Once the butter starts to bubble, spoon the batter onto the skillet. Cook until bubbles form on the surface, flip, and cook until second side is golden brown. Repeat until all the batter is used and add more butter or oil as you go. Reheat the toffee sauce to loosen the consistency if needed and serve immediately with pancakes.

Drizzle the pancakes with the glaze and serve.

Toasted Coconut Cakes with Honey Cardamom Glaze

DIFFICULTY: 2

Toasting the shredded and sweetened coconut is essential in this recipe to achieve the distinct flavor for these pancakes. For the glaze, you can omit the cornstarch for a more liquid glaze that will seep into the pancakes or add more than listed in the recipe to make it your desired thickness.

PANCAKES

1 cup shredded sweetened coconut

2 cups flour

2 tablespoons sugar

2 teaspoons baking powder

1 teaspoon baking soda

½ teaspoon salt

2 cups buttermilk (can use 2 cups whole milk plus 2 tablespoons vinegar)

2 eggs

¼ cup coconut oil, melted

1 teaspoon vanilla

TOPPING

1 cup unsweetened coconut milk

½ teaspoon cinnamon

¼ teaspoon nutmeg

1 teaspoon cornstarch

Preheat oven to 325°. Spread coconut on a baking sheet. Bake 5–7 minutes, tossing once, until coconut is toasted. Remove and set aside.

In a large bowl, whisk flour, sugar, baking powder, soda, and salt. In a small bowl, whisk milk, eggs, oil, and vanilla. Add wet ingredients to flour mixture and stir until just combined, while being careful not to overmix.

Heat griddle or pan to medium-low heat. Coat with cooking spray. Spoon about ⅓ cup batter onto a heated griddle. Sprinkle with toasted coconut. Cook until the surfaces of the pancakes develop some bubbles, about two minutes. Flip and cook until undersides have browned, another two minutes. Continue until batter is gone.

To make sauce, combine all ingredients in a small saucepan and bring to a boil. Boil and whisk continuously for a minute then lower heat to keep warm before serving. If sauce becomes too thick, add more coconut milk.

Serve pancakes topped with warm sauce and additional toasted coconut.

Hummingbird Pancakes
DIFFICULTY: 3

Hummingbird cake is a spice cake flavored with bananas and pineapple and a cream cheese frosting with roots in the southern United States. Our version of the pancake includes a cream cheese flavored pudding. If you prefer not to make pudding from scratch, boxed cook-and-serve vanilla pudding can be used in its place, but don't forget the cream cheese component to achieve the traditional hummingbird flavors!

PANCAKES

1½ cups flour

2 teaspoons baking powder

¾ teaspoon salt

½ teaspoon cinnamon

1½ cups buttermilk

1 cup mashed, ripe bananas

½ cup canned crushed pineapple

⅓ cup sugar

1 egg, beaten

3 tablespoons vegetable oil

½ cup chopped toasted pecans

CREAM CHEESE PUDDING

1½ cups whole milk

4 ounces cream cheese, softened

⅓ cup sugar

3 egg yolks

1 tablespoon cornstarch

⅛ teaspoon salt

2 tablespoons butter

1 teaspoon vanilla

In a large bowl, stir together flour, baking powder, salt, and cinnamon. In another bowl, whisk together buttermilk, banana, pineapple, sugar, egg, and oil. Gradually stir buttermilk mixture into flour mixture until just moistened. Fold in toasted pecans. Heat griddle or skillet over medium heat and butter. Pour ¼ cup batter onto skillet and cook for 3–4 minutes or until tops are covered in bubbles and edges look dry. Flip and cook an additional 3–4 minutes or until done. Keep warm by placing on a plate and cover with foil while cooking additional pancakes.

To make pudding, mix cream cheese, sugar, egg yolks, cornstarch and salt in a stand mixer until combined and smooth. Pour mixture into a medium saucepan over medium heat, whisking constantly. Boil for one minute, still whisking. Remove from heat and stir in butter and vanilla.

Serve pancakes with pudding and sliced bananas, pineapple, and pecans.

Carrot Cakes

DIFFICULTY: 2

Much like the cake this recipe is named for, these carrot cake pancakes are loaded with fresh shredded carrot, bright orange zest, spicy pumpkin pie spice, and the pecans are toasted to add depth of flavor and crunch. Oh, and they are topped with a maple cream cheese glaze to tie the flavors together.

PANCAKES

1½ cups flour

4 tablespoons sugar

1 teaspoon baking powder

1 teaspoon pumpkin pie spice

½ teaspoon baking soda

½ teaspoon salt

2 eggs

1½ cups buttermilk

3 tablespoons butter, melted

½ teaspoon vanilla

1 cup packed finely grated carrot

1 teaspoon orange zest

¼ cup chopped toasted pecans

MAPLE CREAM CHEESE DRIZZLE

8 ounces softened cream cheese

½ cup dark maple syrup

4 tablespoons butter

Whisk together flour, sugar, baking powder, pumpkin pie spice, baking soda, and salt in a large bowl. Whisk together the eggs, buttermilk, melted butter and vanilla in another large bowl. Add the carrots and orange zest and mix until smooth. Add the wet ingredients to the dry ingredients and mix until just combined. Cover and refrigerate for 30 minutes.

Heat a griddle or large skillet. Coat with cooking spray or butter. Spoon ¼ cup batter onto the skillet, spreading with a spatula. Cook until the tops are covered with bubbles and edges look cooked, about two minutes. Flip pancakes and cook until bottoms are lightly browned, about one minute. Repeat until batter is gone. Keep pancakes warm on a plate covered with foil.

To make cream cheese drizzle, combine cream cheese, syrup and butter in a bowl, or the bowl of a stand mixer with the whisk attachment until combined, about two minutes.

Serve pancakes on a plate and drizzle with cream cheese glaze. Top with additional pecans if desired.

Black Forest Pancakes

DIFFICULTY: 2

The cherry compote is what really makes these pancakes. We cut fresh cherries in half and then pulled out the pit. There is a specialized cherry pitting tool, but that is not necessarily needed for this somewhat small amount of cherries. If fresh cherries are not seasonally available, you can skip the compote and use canned cherry pie filling.

CHERRY COMPOTE

12½ ounces dark cherries, pitted

2 tablespoons sugar

¼ teaspoon cinnamon

3 tablespoons water

1 teaspoon cornstarch

PANCAKES

⅓ cup flour

6 tablespoons unsweetened cocoa powder

6 tablespoons sugar

2 teaspoons baking powder

4 eggs, separated

¼ teaspoons salt

1 cup milk

4 tablespoons butter, melted

Whipped cream for serving

In a medium saucepan, bring all the ingredients for the cherry compote to the boil. Stir, cover with a lid and cook on medium heat for 5–7 minutes or until the fruits start to soften. Take the pan off the heat, adjust to taste and pour the compote into a bowl. Let mixture cool.

In a large bowl, combine the flour, cocoa, sugar and baking powder. With a stand mixer, beat the egg whites and salt until stiff and set aside. Whisk the egg yolks, milk, and butter into the dry mixture and mix until well combined. Gently fold in the stiff egg whites. Heat about ½ teaspoon butter in a skillet and pour ¼ cup batter for each pancake. Cook about 1–2 minutes on medium heat, or golden brown, and flip. Cook them in batches of 2–3, always adding ½ teaspoon butter before you start the next round. Stack the cooked pancakes on a plate, serve with whipped cream, cherry compote, sandwiched or separately arranged on plates.

Tiramisu Pancakes

DIFFICULTY: 2

Just like the dessert itself, these pancakes are layer after layer of light, mildly sweet pancakes, mascarpone, and whipped cream filling with hints of cocoa and espresso. To make a stunning pancake dessert, make a tall stack of the pancakes and filling, dust with cocoa powder, serve on a pedestal, and slice.

PANCAKES

2 tablespoons butter, melted

2 eggs

1½ cups milk

1 cup flour

2 teaspoons baking powder

1 teaspoon vanilla extract

FILLING

8 ounces mascarpone (at room temperature)

1 cup heavy whipping cream

¼ cup powdered sugar

2 teaspoons espresso powder

Cocoa powder for topping, optional

In a medium bowl, whisk together the melted butter and eggs. Add the milk and whisk until just combined. Add the remaining ingredients for the pancakes, whisking until the batter is smooth. Heat a griddle or skillet over medium heat. Pour the batter into 3–4-inch rounds, cooking until golden brown on each side.

In another bowl, combine the whipping cream, powdered sugar and espresso powder and whip until soft peaks form. In a separate bowl, beat the mascarpone until smooth. Add the whipping cream and fold together until combined.

Spread a thin layer of the mascarpone filling between each layer of the cooled pancakes and sprinkle with cocoa powder.

Whole Wheat Coffee Pancakes with Mocha Syrup

DIFFICULTY: 2

Don't let the whole wheat deter you from this recipe; the whole wheat flour only adds to the heartiness of the pancakes. Topped with rich mocha syrup that soaks right into them, this is the perfect recipe for any coffee and chocolate-loving adult!

PANCAKES

1¼ cups whole wheat flour

1½ tablespoons instant coffee

1 cup milk

1 teaspoon vinegar or lemon juice

1 egg

1 tablespoon maple syrup

1 tablespoon oil

1 teaspoon pure vanilla extract

1 teaspoon baking soda

¼ teaspoon sea salt

MOCHA SYRUP

1 tablespoon instant coffee

½ cup water

¼ cup sugar

¼ cup cocoa powder

1½ teaspoons vanilla extract

¼ teaspoon salt

In a small saucepan, combine all the syrup ingredients (except vanilla) and bring to a simmer. Stir until syrup begins to thicken, about 7–10 minutes. Turn off the heat and stir in vanilla extract.

In a bowl, mix together milk and vinegar. Let it curdle. In a separate bowl, whisk together instant coffee, flour, baking soda and salt. Add egg, maple syrup, oil, and vanilla to milk mixture. Add wet mixture to dry mixture and stir until just combined.

Heat a pan or skillet over medium heat and lightly grease. Pour ¼ cup batter and cook until you see bubbles, flip the pancake and cook the other side (about 2 minutes per side). Repeat with the remaining batter, and top finished pancakes with healthy dose of mocha syrup.

Salted Caramel Stuffed Silver Dollars

DIFFICULTY: 2

Sea salt is one of the best things to have happened to caramel, and salted caramel may be one of the best things to have happened to pancakes. We kept these pancakes at a small size because they are really two pancakes sandwiched together. A little bit of caramel may ooze out of the sides of the pancakes as it heats up.

3 eggs

½ cup sugar

½ cup milk

1 tablespoon vinegar

2 teaspoons baking powder

1½ cups flour

¼ cup butter, melted

1 tablespoon maple syrup

Oil, for greasing

Premade salted caramel sauce

In a medium bowl, stir together milk and vinegar until curdled. Whisk in the sugar, maple syrup, butter and eggs. In a separate bowl, stir together flour and baking soda. Add the wet ingredients to the dry ingredients and stir until just combined.

Heat a large pan or griddle over medium heat. Lightly grease. Add two tablespoons of the batter to the frying pan in multiples of two. Once pancakes have formed bubbles and are nearly dry, add one heaped teaspoon of the salted caramel to every other pancake. Flip the non-caramel pancake onto the pancake topped with caramel to create a sandwich. Let cook for an additional minute or until cooked through on the edges.

Cannoli Pancakes

DIFFICULTY: 3

Cannoli are a tasty treat on their own, but take that rich and creamy filling studded with dark mini-chocolate chips and put it in between a pancake or two, and you're in heaven. You can spread the filling in between stacked pancakes or in the center of one pancake and fold it over. The cannoli filling can be stored in the fridge for up to two weeks.

FILLING

8 ounces whole milk ricotta cheese, drained and dried

8 ounces mascarpone cheese, softened

1 teaspoon vanilla

1½ cups powdered sugar

¼ teaspoon salt

¾ cup chocolate chips

PANCAKES

2 eggs

2 cups buttermilk

4 tablespoons butter, melted

½ teaspoon vanilla

2 cups flour

3 tablespoons sugar

2 teaspoons baking powder

1 teaspoon baking soda

1 teaspoon salt

In the bowl of a stand mixer fitted with the whisk attachment or a large mixing bowl with an electric mixer, beat mascarpone until light and fluffy. Add dry ricotta cheese, whisking until fully combined, approximately 2–3 minutes. Squeeze ricotta in cheesecloth to ensure all excess liquid is removed. Add vanilla and powdered sugar. Fold in chocolate chips. Refrigerate until after you make the pancakes.

In a large mixing bowl, whisk eggs. Add buttermilk, melted butter and vanilla, whisking until combined.

In a separate mixing bowl, whisk together flour, sugar, baking powder, baking soda and salt.

Gradually add dry ingredients to wet ingredients until just combined. Do not overmix. Batter will be lumpy.

Heat a skillet or griddle over medium heat. Grease well and pour in pancake batter. Size is up to you, however if you want to fold your cannoli pancakes like I did in the picture, aim for a diameter of about 8 inches. You can also make smaller pancakes and stack them with filling between each layer. When air bubbles appear, flip pancakes. Remove cannoli filling from the fridge. Top pancakes, fold pancakes or layer pancakes with cannoli filling. Garnish with your choice of powdered sugar or chocolate chips.

Brownie Batter Pancakes

DIFFICULTY: 1

This is most definitely the recipe for the extreme chocolate lover! Pancakes that taste just like a brownie, that come together quickly. The added richness of the chocolate chips is cut by topping the stack with vanilla (or chocolate) ice cream.

1 cup flour

1¼ cups brownie mix (any style/brand)

1 teaspoon baking powder

1 teaspoon baking soda

½ teaspoon salt

2 eggs

1 cup milk

1 teaspoon vanilla

½ cup chocolate chips

Rainbow sprinkles, for serving (optional)

Vanilla ice cream, for serving (optional)

In a large bowl, whisk together flour, brownie mix, baking powder, baking soda and salt. Beat in eggs, milk and vanilla. Fold in chocolate chips.

Heat a large skillet or griddle over medium heat. Grease and then spoon about ⅓ cup pancake batter into the pan. When little bubbles appear, flip and cook through (about 1–2 minutes). Cook until browned on both sides.

Top with sprinkles and a big scoop of ice cream. Serve immediately.

Maple Bar Pancakes

DIFFICULTY: 1

Pancakes, but in bar form! These are essentially classic buttermilk pancakes in a fun shape, topped with a decadent maple glaze instead of plain maple syrup. If you have maple cream on hand, that works just as well for the glaze.

MAPLE GLAZE

¼ cup butter, melted

1½ cups powdered sugar

½ teaspoon maple syrup

¼ cup whole milk

1 teaspoon vanilla

PANCAKES

1 teaspoon salt

2 teaspoons baking powder

1 teaspoon baking soda

2 cups flour

2 tablespoons sugar

2 eggs, beaten

2 cups buttermilk

2 tablespoons butter, melted

To make the glaze, in a small bowl, whisk together the butter, powdered sugar, maple syrup, milk, and vanilla until smooth. Set aside.

To make the pancakes, preheat griddle to medium heat. In a medium bowl, whisk together salt, baking powder, baking soda, flour and sugar. In a separate medium bowl, whisk together the eggs and buttermilk, whisk in the melted butter. Make a well in the center of the dry ingredients. Pour in the wet ingredients and stir until just combined, being careful not to overmix.

Butter the hot griddle and scoop ⅓ cup batter, pouring it into a bar-like shape. Cook until bubbles begin to form and underside is golden brown. Flip and cook until second side is golden. Continue with the remaining batter. Spread glaze over each pancake and serve.

Hot Cocoa Pancakes

DIFFICULTY: 1

Nothing like a batch of hot cocoa pancakes to warm up with after a day of winter fun. What makes these pancakes even better is the marshmallow dolloped on top. We used the microwave to melt the marshmallows, but placing them on the pancakes and putting them under the broiler for a few minutes can get them nice and toasted.

1 cup buttermilk

1 cup flour

2 teaspoons baking powder

¼ cup + 2 tablespoons cocoa powder, divided

½ teaspoons cinnamon

Pinch of salt

3 tablespoons maple syrup

¼ cup oil (coconut or canola works best)

1½ teaspoons vanilla

1 cup marshmallows (or fluff) for topping, optional

Mix the flour, baking powder, cocoa powder, cinnamon and salt together in a large bowl until combined. Add the buttermilk, maple syrup, coconut oil and vanilla. Mix with a wooden spoon until just combined.

Heat a skillet or pan over medium heat. Drop ¼ cup measures of the batter into the pan. When bubbles start to peak through the surface and you see a bit of light browning/crisping up on the underside, flip the pancakes over carefully, about 1–2 minutes. Repeat for the other side.

If using marshmallows, microwave for 10–15 seconds until soft and spread over pancakes. Finish with sifting of cocoa powder.

A Pancake
By Any
Other Name

While obsessing over pancakes, we again and again pushed the boundaries of the standard flapjack. This chapter includes pancakes in other forms, without straying too far from the true conception. A number of the recipes in this chapter lend themselves well to a crowd, namely the blueberry pancake casserole and the sheet pan pancake. When complete, our reactions ranged from, "Wow, this is really cool!" to "What an interesting concept!" and, "What amazing flavor!" We decided that's exactly what cooks want to hear in a room full of guests!

Two-Way Sweet Potato "Pancakes"

DIFFICULTY: 2

Sweet potatoes are a great source of fiber, vitamins, and minerals, and are versatile in both sweet and savory dishes. For a savory take on these waffles or pancakes, just omit the ground cinnamon.on top.

2 cups mashed sweet potato (boiled until soft, skin removed)

2 large eggs

Pinch of salt

⅛ teaspoons ground cinnamon

3 tablespoons flour

Maple syrup (for serving)

Walnuts (for serving)

Pre-heat a waffle iron to medium-high heat and spray with cooking spray.

Combine all ingredients in a mixing bowl until smooth. If making pancakes, just double the amount of flour.

Fill your waffle maker to capacity. Cook the waffles according to the instructions of your waffle maker, perhaps a bit longer. Sweet potatoes take additional time to brown and crisp. Serve with a little maple syrup and walnuts.

Pancake Muffins

DIFFICULTY: 2

Muffins are the perfect grab and go breakfast or snack, and these ones are even better because they taste just like a pancake! In our version we used three types of berry, but you can use just one variety or even bananas, nuts, or chocolate chips.

MUFFINS

⅓ cup whole milk

1 egg

1 egg yolk

1 tablespoon pure maple syrup

1 teaspoon vanilla

7 tablespoons salted butter, melted and slightly cooled

1½ cups flour

½ cup sugar

1½ teaspoons baking powder

½ teaspoon salt

½ cup fresh berries (blueberries, blackberries, raspberries, or all three)

GLAZE

¾ cup pure maple syrup

1 tablespoon butter, melted

1 teaspoon vanilla

Preheat oven to 375°F with a rack in the center. Line a muffin tin with paper liners.

In another bowl, whisk flour, sugar, baking powder and salt. Add the milk mixture and gently stir. Fold in berries. Divide batter into prepared muffin tin. Bake muffins until golden and a toothpick inserted into the center comes out clean, around 18–22 minutes.

To make the glaze, combine ingredients in a small bowl. Poke several holes into warm muffins with a toothpick and drizzle a spoonful of syrup over each muffin.

Pancake Bread

DIFFICULTY: 2

This light, buttery, and irresistible take on a pancake is even better when served warm with butter. While it might not be deemed a "quick bread", it's well worth the wait.

TOPPING

¼ teaspoon cinnamon

1 tablespoon butter, room temp

2 tablespoons flour

2 tablespoons brown sugar

Pinch of salt

BREAD

Cooking spray (for pan)

1 stick butter, room temp

2 cups flour

1 cup packed brown sugar

¼ teaspoon salt

1 teaspoon baking soda

½ teaspoon baking powder

1 cup sour cream

⅔ cup maple syrup

2 teaspoons vanilla

2 eggs

Position a rack in the center of oven and preheat to 350°. Line a 9x5-inch loaf pan with parchment and spray with cooking spray. With a fork, smash cinnamon, butter, flour, brown sugar and salt in a small bowl until combined and lumps form. Set aside.

Whisk together the baking soda, baking powder, flour and salt in a medium bowl until combined. Whisk together the sour cream, syrup, and vanilla in a small bowl until combined and smooth. Beat butter in a large bowl with an electric mixer on medium-high speed until light and creamy, about 3 minutes. Gradually add the brown sugar and beat 3 minutes more, until light and fluffy. Add the eggs, one at a time, beating until fully incorporated. Continue to beat until the mixture is light and fluffy, about 1 minute. Reduce speed to low and add the dry ingredients in three additions, alternating with the wet ingredients, beginning and ending with the dry ingredients. Scrape the batter into the prepared loaf pan and smooth the top. Sprinkle with the crumb topping.

Bake until the top is brown and a tester inserted into the center comes out clean, about 1 hour. Let the bread sit in the pan for about 5 minutes, then remove it from the pan and cool on a wire rack for about 30 minutes before slicing. Serve warm with butter.

Blueberry Pancake Casserole

DIFFICULTY: 2

This is a great recipe for a crowd and can be made fairly quick. Feel free to substitute other berries for the blueberries or add different ones for a mixed berry take. Adding toasted nuts to the crumble topping if desired, will add an extra element of crunch.

Pancakes Make People Happy

CRUMB TOPPING

½ cup flour

3 tablespoons brown sugar

2 tablespoons sugar

½ teaspoon cinnamon

¼ teaspoon salt

4 tablespoons butter, melted

CASSEROLE

2½ cups flour

2 tablespoons sugar

½ teaspoon salt

1 teaspoon baking powder

1 teaspoon baking soda

2 eggs

2 cups buttermilk

½ cup milk

¼ cup butter, melted

Finely grated zest of 1 small lemon

1½ teaspoons vanilla

1⅔ cups blueberries

Maple syrup, for serving

Preheat oven to 350°F. Thoroughly grease a 9x13-inch baking dish and set aside. To prepare crumb topping, combine flour, sugars, cinnamon, and salt. Add melted butter and stir until fully incorporated. Cover and refrigerate while you prepare the batter.

In a large bowl, combine flour, sugar, salt, baking powder, and baking soda.

Bake until the top is brown and a tester inserted into the center comes out clean, about 1 hour. Let the bread sit in the pan for about 5 minutes, then remove it from the pan and cool on a wire rack for about 30 minutes before slicing. Serve warm with butter.

Sheet Pan Pancakes

DIFFICULTY: 1

One of the easiest recipes in this book, and easily one of the most crowd-pleasing. Top these pancake with everyone's favorite topping, be it chocolate chips, berries, nuts, jam, etc., and bake. An easy and simple solution to busy mornings.

Pancakes Make People Happy

2 cups flour

⅓ cup confectioner's
   sugar

⅔ cup cornstarch

4 teaspoons baking
   powder

½ teaspoon salt

2 eggs

2 cups buttermilk

1½ teaspoons vanilla

5 tablespoons butter,
   melted

¼ cup favorite jam
   (preferably a loose,
   runny jam)

Line a sheet pan (about 18x13-inch) with parchment paper and brush the bottom with 1 tablespoon butter or spray with nonstick spray.

Preheat oven to 425°F. In a large mixing bowl, combine flour, confectioner's sugar, cornstarch, baking powder and salt.

In a separate bowl, combine eggs, buttermilk, vanilla and melted butter and mix well. Pour the wet ingredients into the dry ingredients and mix until just combined. Do not overmix. Scrape the batter into the prepared sheet pan, and then evenly spread the batter.

Take your jam (if you do not have loose jam, you can also heat your jam in the microwave for a few seconds to loosen it) and use a spoon to drizzle lines over the batter across the sheet pan. Take a knife and drag across the top of the batter perpendicular to your jam lines to create a design.

Place the sheet pan in the center of your oven and bake for 6–8 minutes. Check at 5 minutes: the pancakes are done if the center of the pancake is springy to the touch and a toothpick inserted into the middle comes out clean. Serve immediately. If you end up with any leftovers, it's best to freeze them and reheat when it's time to enjoy.

Cardamom Bun Pancakes
with Honey Butter

DIFFICULTY: 3

Because these are made with a yeasted dough, they resemble the consistency of an English muffin, and pair well with honey and butter. Vegetable oil can be substituted for the coconut oil.

1¼ cups spelt flour (can substitute white flour)

½ cup oat flour*

1 packet dry yeast

¼ cup sugar + ¼ cup for coating after

1 teaspoon ground cardamom

½ teaspoon salt

½ cup yogurt

¼ cup sour cream

3 tablespoons water

3 tablespoons coconut oil, melted (plus more for frying)

1 tablespoon honey

3 tablespoons butter

If you don't have oat flour, all you need to do is throw ½ cup rolled oats in a blender or food processor!

In a large bowl, mix together the dry ingredients: flours, yeast, sugar, cardamom and salt. In a small saucepan, mix yogurt, sour cream and water and heat until steaming, but not bubbling. Turn off heat. Using a spatula, pour and scrape heated mixture into dry ingredients and stir to combine. Add melted coconut oil and knead for a few minutes.

Cover the bowl with a tea towel and let rise for about 30 minutes. While the dough is rising, you can whip together your honey and butter with a hand mixer and set aside.

From this point, you can either scoop small amounts of the batter out with your hands, roll into a ball, and flatten into a small, thick pancake shape, or dump the whole batter onto a floured surface, roll out, and divide equally before rolling into balls and flattening.

Melt coconut oil in a pan and fry each bun pancake about 1–2 minutes per side on medium heat, until sides appear browned and pancakes hold steady when you gently push on them.

While still warm, brush coconut oil on each side and dip in sugar. Serve warm topped with honey butter. (They're also excellent the next day, after microwaving and topping with butter.)

Blueberry Pancake Ice Cream

DIFFICULTY: 4

Blueberry pancakes with butter and maple syrup are typically enjoyed at breakfast, but this rich and creamy ice cream is the perfect dessert. While you won't be able to enjoy it on the same day, a homemade ice cream is worth the wait! Feel free to make extra blueberry compote to use as a topping. Note: An ice cream maker is required for this recipe.

ICE CREAM BASE

1½ cups whole milk

1½ cups heavy cream

4 egg yolks

1 teaspoon vanilla

½ cup maple syrup

¼ cup sugar

1 tablespoon butter

½ teaspoon salt

BLUEBERRY COMPOTE

1½ cups fresh blueberries

¼ cup sugar

Juice from ½ lemon

Whisk egg yolks in a medium bowl until bubbly, and set aside. In a large saucepan, combine milk, maple syrup and sugar. With a wooden spoon, stir the mixture over medium-low heat until just about to bubble, stirring the entire time. Temper the yolks by adding about ¼ cup hot milk mixture into the yolk mixture, stirring until combined. Pour the egg mixture into the saucepan with the milk mixture, stirring until mixture is fully incorporated.

Continue cooking the mixture, stirring, on low heat, until it begins to thicken, about 5 minutes. Remove from heat and stir in heavy cream, vanilla, butter, and salt. Stir until butter is melted. Pour mixture into freezer-safe container and place in freezer for 1–2 hours, or until mixture begins to freeze around the sides.

Once chilled, pour ice cream mixture into ice cream maker and churn according to manufacturer's directions.

While ice cream is churning, combine blueberry compote ingredients in a small saucepan over medium heat. Cook until blueberries are about ready to burst. Remove from heat and chill.

When churned, scoop ice cream mixture into a container. Pour blueberry compote over ice cream mixture and gently swirl. Do not stir in compote unless a completely blue ice cream is desired. Place the container in the freezer overnight or at least 12 hours. Scoop and serve.

Closing Words

So, there you have it: a comprehensive collection of pancake recipes to impress family, friends and neighbors. We suggest a weekend pancake buffet—it happened more than once while we were creating the book and it was delightful! Just add balloons and you have the perfect party for children or adults.

And why? Why does a table full of easy-to-make, easy-to-eat pancakes bring everyone crowding around, asking for seconds and thirds? It's simple.

Because pancakes make people happy!

About the Authors

Sharon Collins is a Catskills Mountains native and lifelong farmer. She grew up on a dairy farm and transitioned to a pure maple syrup and specialty food manufacturer in 1990. She is a pioneer in the value-added product business. Her fascination with homegrown and locally produced seasonal products has fueled her entire business model as the owner and operator of Buck Hill Farm. She developed a diversified homestead into a year-round agritourism destination. The farm serves full country breakfast every weekend, all year, featuring home-raised pastured pork, beef, eggs and the farm's own pancake mixes.

Charlotte Collins is a third-generation farmer in the Northern Catskills of Upstate NY. She has been on a plant-based diet for over 12 years which has inspired much of her interest in creative cooking. With a degree in direct marketing and multiple fitness certifications, she focuses on communicating the physical and economic benefits of consuming locally produced goods. Charlotte lived in New York City for 6 years working in fitness instructing, PR, and sales before returning to her family farm, Buck Hill Farm.

Courtney Wade, author of the Catskills Farm to Table Cookbook, lives on a farm in the Catskills Mountain region of New York and has an intense passion for farm fresh food. With both a degree in graphic design and agricultural business from the State University at Cobleskill, she understands the importance of and promotes supporting local producers by purchasing seasonally grown products.

About Buck Hill Farm

Anyone living in the small town of Jefferson, New York knows that the best place for breakfast on the weekends is at Buck Hill Farm. Vehicles of locals and visitors alike will quickly fill the driveway and line both sides of the road on Saturday and Sunday mornings.

Buck Hill Farm was originally owned and operated by Sharon's parents, Charles and Lynn Buck, who quickly established high standards by producing consistently good maple syrup the most efficient way they knew how. Buck Hill Farm became one of the first farms to market their products at the Greenmarkets in New York City in the mid-1970s. For the next two decades, they worked hard to increase their syrup production and introduced a value-added product line that featured condiments and pancake mixes.

Sharon and her family continued to grow the farm by creating a large wholesale business, servicing restaurants, farm stands, and groceries, all the while still taking products to the Greenmarkets in NYC. In 1995, the sap-house kitchen was renovated and the now-renowned Saturday and Sunday breakfasts began being served. The value-added product line was also expanded to include snacks, cereals, and maple pickles!

In recent years, Buck Hill's business model has been re-developed to emphasize sustainable practices. This includes eliminating long-distance deliveries, maximizing production from the land on the farm, and locally sourcing as many supplies as possible.

Buck Hill Farm pioneered the farm to table concept. They offered on-farm dining and an array of products made from their own land well before the popular term was even coined.. If it isn't made, raised, grown, or collected on the farm, it is most certainly sourced locally. The eggs, bacon, sausage and ham found on the menu are all sourced from the farm; beets, cucumbers and tomatoes grown in our gardens are used to make value-added products sold at the store; apples and berries foraged on the farm are used to make applesauce and unique products like elderberry elixir and blackberry tonic.

It doesn't matter if it is your first or hundredth visit, a trip to Buck Hill Farm leaves a lasting impression. There is a reason why cars line up on the weekends, even on a back road in a small town in the Catskills. Whether it's watching maple syrup being made, exploring the gardens, meeting the farm animals, or enjoying a Catskills farm to table breakfast, Buck Hill Farm strives to make visitors feel like family. With just one visit you will realize why they say, "You're not going out for breakfast; you're coming over for breakfast." Throughout the years, in spite of the growth and changes, the farm's core has always been its customers. We believe sharing the farm experience with visitors is the most important thing we do. Visit us at buckhillfarm.com.

Index

A

Apple Cider Pancakes with Caramel Apple Syrup **98**

Apple Crisp Topped Pancakes **118**

Austrian Torn Fluffy Pancake (Kaiserschmarrn) **88**

Avocado Pancakes **62**

B

Bacon & Salted Honey Pancake **60**

Banana Bread Pancakes with Caramelized Bananas **16**

Basil Orange Ricotta Cakes **38**

Berry Ombre Pancakes **116**

Black Forest Pancakes **136**

Blueberry Pancake Casserole **160**

Blueberry Pancake Ice Cream **166**

Brownie Batter Pancakes **146**

Brunchy Dutch Baby **52**

Buckwheat Galettes **34**

Buckwheat Pancakes **6**

Butternut Griddle Biscuits with Sage Brown Butter **104**

C

Cabbage Pancakes **30**

Cachapa (Venezuelan Corn Pancakes) **80**

Cannoli Pancakes **144**

Cardamom Bun Pancakes with Honey Butter **164**

Carrot Cakes **134**

Chickpea Pancakes with Broccoli Rabe & Roasted Chickpeas **42**

Christmas Tree Stack **110**

Cinnamon Roll Pancakes **126**

Cinnamon Toast Crunch™ Cakes **66**

Citrus Mimosa Pancakes **64**

Cornmeal Cakes **14**

Cornmeal Cakes with Green Tomato Chutney **112**

Cranberry Rum Pancakes with Butter Rum Syrup **54**

Crispy Risotto Pancake **32**

Crunchy Granola Pancakes with Blackberry Butter **56**

E

Eggnog Pancakes **100**

Einkorn Cakes **22**

F

Farinata **92**

Fluffy Lemon Ricotta Pancakes **10**

Funfetti Pancakes **122**

G

Guinness Pancakes **70**

H

Hardy Polenta Cakes **18**

Hot Cocoa Pancakes **150**

Hummingbird Pancakes **132**

I

Indian Chai Spice Pancakes with Black Tea
Poached Pear **90**

J

Jalapeño Corn Fritter Pancakes **28**
Japanese Souffle Pancakes **76**

K

Kimchi Pancakes **46**
Korean Shrimp Pancakes **84**

L

Leftover Herbed Smashed Potato
Pancakes **8**
Lemon Poppyseed Pancakes **124**
Lofty Gingerbread Pancakes **102**

M

Malaysian Peanut Pancake Turnover
(Apam Balik) **86**
Maple Bar Pancakes **148**
Mini German Apple Pancakes **74**
Monte Cristo Pancakes **58**

O

Old Fashioned Buttermilk Pancakes **4**

P

Pancake Bread **158**
Pancake Muffins **156**
Peachy Summer Dutch Baby **108**
Peanut Butter Pancakes with Four Berry
Compote **12**

Pink Heart Beet Pancakes **106**
Pistachio Pancakes with Pistachio Chevre **44**
Pumpkin Pancakes with Maple Roasted
Walnuts **96**

R

Red, White, & Blue Pancakes **114**

S

Salted Caramel Stuffed Silver Dollars **142**
Scottish Oat Cakes **78**
Sheet Pan Pancakes **162**
Shou Zhua Bing Chinese Pancakes **82**
Sour Cream Pancakes **20**
Spinach Pancakes **40**
Squash & Eggplant Pancakes with Pickled
Red Onions **48**
Sticky Toffee Pancakes **128**

T

Tiramisu Pancakes **138**
Toasted Coconut Cakes with Honey
Cardamom Glaze **130**
Two-Way Sweet Potato "Pancakes" **154**

W

Whipped Saffron & Pea Cakes **36**
White Cheddar Zucchini Cakes with Honey
and Rosemary **26**
Wholesome Sunflower Pancakes with Maple
Bourbon Berries **68**
Whole Wheat Coffee Pancakes with Mocha
Syrup **140**